WHY THE CAKE WON'T RISE

AND THE JELLY WON'T SET

WHY THE CAKE WON'T RISE

WON'T RISE

AND THE JELLY WON'T SET

A Complete Guide to Avoiding Kitchen Failures

Kathleen Thorne-Thomsen

Linda Brownridge

A & W Publishers, Inc.
New York

For James and Edward

We appreciate the many hours that Rosa Hamilton,
Rebecca Newman, Shari Shepherd, and Peggy Wilson
spent reading, researching, and commenting on our
manuscript and illustrations.
   We are indebted to Peri Winkler, our literary agent, for
her support and excellent management.
   We would also like to thank all of our friends who
tasted, tested, judged, and gained weight over this
venture.

Published by
A & W Publishers, Inc.
95 Madison Avenue
New York, New York 10016

Library of Congress Cataloging in Publication Data

Thorne-Thomsen, Kathleen.
   Why the cake won't rise and the jelly won't set.

   Bibliography: p.
   Includes index.
   1. Cookery. I. Brownridge, Linda, joint
author. II. Title.
TX652.T46   641.5   78-69996
ISBN 0-89479-036-6

Designed by Helen Roberts and Kathleen Thorne-Thomsen

Illustrations by Linda Brownridge

Printed in the United States of America

Table of Contents

Introduction

This book is for everyone who has ever tried with the best of intentions to bake a loaf of bread, cook a hollandaise sauce, or make any other homemade kitchen specialty. Through no fault of your own, and for all the reasons you didn't understand because they weren't included in the recipe, your efforts resulted in dismal failure. This experience at the least discouraged you, and at the worst was a possible embarrassment at a carefully planned dinner party. After one or two of these experiences, you may not be willing to risk baking bread or making hollandaise sauce again. We have written this book especially for you. If you follow our recipes exactly, and read the kitchen procedures section carefully, you should produce perfect results with each effort.

We are not attempting in this book to cover every area of cooking, for we feel there are many excellent sources for meat, vegetable, and fruit recipes, which can in general be prepared more simply. We are concentrating instead on foods that repeatedly cause the most problems: baked products, egg dishes, and sauces made from varying amounts of the same basic ingredients: flour, sugar, eggs, liquids, fat, a leavening agent, salt, and other flavorings. We have also included a few extra goodies, like jelly and jam, which cause problems for similar reasons though they utilize only one of the basic ingredients. When a combination of these ingredients is mixed together and cooked, a complex chemical reaction occurs. This reaction may be seriously impaired by improper mixing and cooking procedures. When the ingredients are combined and cooked the correct way, you should have perfect results each time.

We begin the book with a brief discussion of the ingredients. It is important that you carefully read this section, because, as an example, there are at least five different kinds of white flour commercially available to you. We will use each of them at different times in the book, and we want you to understand the differences. The ingredients section also has information on measurements, equivalents, and acceptable substitutions.

The kitchen procedures section describes how to measure ingredients. It is absolutely necessary to read this section, for you must learn to measure ingredients correctly if you are to avoid kitchen failures. It also gives tips for successful cooking and baking.

We have organized the recipe section of the book into eight sections. These sections are listed in the table of contents. You may find our grouping of recipes is different from those in other cookbooks you have used. We have deliberately done this to help you understand the underlying principles of each recipe. We hope it will be easier to learn the principles by association with similarities in cooking other foods. All of the recipes are listed in the index at the back of the book.

Finally, we hope you will like our recipes well enough to use them often. Before you experiment with a new recipe from a different source, that you suspect may be potentially troublesome, check the directions against our basic procedures. You will find it helpful. Good cooking!

Ingredients

Basic Ingredients

Flour

Wheat flour is the fundamental ingredient in all baked products made from a batter or dough. When it is mixed with a liquid it has the unique ability to form a mixture which sticks together. This happens because of a protein complex called gluten. Gluten forms the primary structural framework of all baked products containing flour.

The amount of flour used in a recipe influences both the size and tenderness of the finished product. Too much flour will cause the baked product to be more dense and somewhat tough; too little flour will result in an undersize finished product. Sifted and unsifted flours do not measure the same. Carefully read through the procedures for sifting and measuring flour described on page 22. Follow them faithfully for the best results.

There are seven or eight different types of flour commercially available at the local supermarket. They are all different, and each has a specific use. The following brief descriptions will be helpful in understanding the differences between these flours.

Unbleached white flour It is milled from a spring-grown hard wheat and has a creamy white appearance and a gritty feeling when rubbed between the fingers. It will not hold a shape when pressed in the hand. Mixed with a liquid this is the most cohesive flour because it contains more gluten than other wheat flours. Hard wheat, grown in climates with mild winters, will be stickier than its cold-winter counterpart.
□ Use unbleached white flour for yeast breads.

Cake flour It is milled from winter soft wheat and is whiter than hard-wheat flour and has a smooth, fine, starchy feel when rubbed between the fingers. It will hold a shape when pressed in the hand. Cake flour has a lower percentage of gluten. Mixed with water it will make a light, porous mixture that is better suited for combining with baking powder or baking soda.
□ Use cake flour in cakes and pastry crusts.

Pastry flour This is a soft-wheat flour formulated especially for pastry crusts. It is usually available only to commercial bakers but may be found in the health food section of some food stores.
□ Use pastry flour in pastry crusts.

Bleached, all-purpose flour This is a blend of hard and soft wheats and is intended for general kitchen usage.
□ Use bleached, all-purpose flour for quick breads, cookies, pastry crusts, and some cakes. It is not suitable for yeast-raised breads.

Instant flour It is a very finely milled all-purpose flour which will easily dissolve in a liquid with a minimum of lumping.
□ Not recommended.

Whole-wheat or graham flour It is a heavy, flavorful flour milled from the whole kernel of wheat, as implied by its name. It has a lower percentage of gluten and should be used in combination with other flours, usually unbleached white or bleached all-purpose flour. Whole-wheat flour is never sifted.

□ Use whole-wheat flour in yeast breads and in many health-food recipes for other baked products.

Rye flour This is another heavy, flavorful low-gluten flour milled from a different grain. It should also be used in combination with a high-gluten flour, usually unbleached white flour.

□ Use in yeast breads.

Self-rising flour This is an all-purpose flour which contains baking soda, salt, and an acid (monocalcium phosphate). We do not recommend using it except where specifically called for in a recipe. If you have no choice but to use self-rising flour to replace all-purpose flour, subtract ½ teaspoon salt and 1½ teaspoons baking powder from the given amounts for every cup of self-rising flour used.

□ Not recommended.

Wheat germ It is the centermost part of a grain of wheat and contains valuable vitamins and some fat. The germ is usually milled out of the wheat because the presence of the fat limits storage life.

□ Use as a nutritional supplement in both yeast and quick breads.

Other Grains

Grains other than those derived from wheat or rye are described here briefly. We have used some of them in this book.

Oat flour contains no gluten. Must be used in combination with wheat flour.

Rice flour contains no gluten. Must be used in combination with wheat flour.

Buckwheat flour contains small amounts of gluten. Used alone it is suitable only for pancakes.

Oatmeal contains no gluten. Must be used in combination with wheat flour.

Rolled oats are processed by steaming and rolling the oat grains. This is the most common commercial oatmeal. Steel-cut oats are processed by cutting the oat grains.

Cornmeal contains no gluten. Must be combined with wheat flour or eggs.

Northern corn bread is baked with yellow cornmeal, which is milled from flint corn grown throughout the North. Southern corn bread is made with Boone County white cornmeal. Boone County white corn is grown in the South.

□ In general these grains are soluble only in hot water. When they are mixed with cold water, the presence of sugar or fat is necessary to separate the starch particles and make a smooth paste.

Sugar

Sugar is an important ingredient in homemade products. Flavor is its most obvious contribution. Sugar also affects the gluten structure of flour, increasing both the tenderness and size of the finished product. Increasing amounts of sugar is beneficial only to a limit. After this point has been reached, the addition of sugar will have an adverse effect and cause the baked product to lose its size, or "fall."

Sugar is responsible for the beautiful golden color of baked products. The brown color is the result of caramelization (the darkening of sugar as it is heated to high temperatures) of the sugar by the dry oven heat.

Sugar also supplies the food which permits yeast to grow in yeast doughs.

Generally speaking white and brown sugars can be used interchangeably. Before making any sugar substitutions, consult the substitutions guide on page 18, and be sure to take the flavor and texture changes into consideration. For example, an angel food cake made with a sugar other than powdered sugar or superfine

sugar will not achieve the same height and lightness as the cake made with powdered sugar.

The following sugars and syrups are available at the local supermarket. The percentage following each name gives the comparative sweetness of each, setting a standard in which white sugar is equal to 100%.

Granulated white sugar (100%) This is the most widely used sweetening substance. It is refined from either sugar cane or sugar beets. Sugars derived from either source are identical chemically. Granulated sugar is available in several granule sizes.

Powdered sugar (100%) It is simply pulverized white sugar to which a small amount of cornstarch has been added. The cornstarch prevents the powdered sugar from caking.

Brown sugar (100%) It has a distinctive and pleasing taste and is partially refined white sugar that still contains a small amount of molasses. Light brown sugar contains less molasses; dark brown sugar contains more molasses.

Honey (97%) This is produced by the honey bee. It is made from the nectar of flowering plants, and the plant determines the flavor of the honey.

Molasses (74%) It is the liquid left after the crystals of sugar are removed from sugar cane. Since the crystals are removed in several stages, there are different flavors of molasses depending on the stage of sugar refinement the molasses is derived from. Light molasses has the mildest flavor; black strap, the strongest flavor. Sorghum molasses is extracted from Chinese sugar cane and has a distinctly different flavor.

Maple sugar or syrup (64%) It is made from the sap of the sugar maple tree.

Corn syrup (30%) This is made from processed cornstarch.

Leavening Agents
Baked products are leavened or raised in a variety of ways.

Air This is present in all baked products. The significance of air as a leavening agent varies. It is most important in egg foams (the trapping of air bubbles in egg whites, egg yolks, or whole eggs through beating) and when incorporated into a fat and sugar during the creaming process.

Steam This is also present in all baked products; the liquid in the batter or dough is converted to steam while baking. The importance of steam as a leavening agent increases directly with the proportion of liquid in the batter.

Yeast This is the leavening agent most widely used to raise

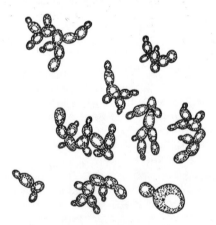

our everyday breads. It is composed of a multitude of tiny one-celled plants that produce carbon dioxide as they multiply. Carbon dioxide is a gas that, as it rises, causes expansion of the cell walls

in the baked product and holds them there until the structure is set by coagulation of the protein.

Baking soda This is familiar to most households. It is used for many purposes other than leavening. When baking soda is moistened in a batter or dough that contains an acid, a chemical reaction occurs and carbon dioxide is produced. The most common acids used in combination with baking soda are vinegar, buttermilk, sour milk, chocolate, molasses, and fruit juices. The reaction between the baking soda and the acid happens quickly, and the batter or dough should be baked immediately after mixing.

Baking powder This is a packaged mixture of baking soda and an acid, usually cream of tartar. The development of commercial baking powder made leavening possible in the multitude of recipes which do not include an acid ingredient, yeast, or an egg foam. When wet by a liquid, the baking soda and acid components of baking powder combine and produce carbon dioxide. The speed at which this reaction occurs is different for each of the three kinds of commercial baking powder. All recipes in this book are based on double-acting baking powder, which releases one-third of its gas immediately at room temperature and two-thirds when heated in the oven.

Liquids
In these homemade products, the most frequently used liquids are water, milk, and cream. These liquids are important because they wet or moisten the dry ingredients. This helps develop the gluten in the flour and causes the leavening agents to act. Liquids

also produce steam, another leavening agent, during the baking process.

Baked products mixed with water have a crisper crust and a more earthy flavor. Baked products mixed with milk have a browner crust and are more flavorful and nutritious.

Milk and cream are available in a variety of forms. These brief descriptions will be helpful in understanding the differences.

Whole milk It is cow's milk containing approximately 3.25% butterfat and 8.25% nonfat milk solids and is usually pasteurized to kill disease-causing bacteria and homogenized to distribute the butterfat evenly throughout the liquid.

Low-fat milk It is whole milk from which all but 2% butterfat has been removed and is somewhat thinner than whole milk.

Skimmed milk It is whole milk from which all the butterfat has been removed. It is very thin and less flavorful than whole milk.

Evaporated milk It is whole milk from which more than half the water content has been removed by evaporation. The flavor is somewhat affected by the heat used in the evaporation process.

Sweetened condensed milk It is whole milk condensed by evaporating half the water and adding sugar to make the milk very thick and sweet.

Dry milk It is whole milk which is vacuum-dried into a powder and has a poor flavor when used alone. It is best used in combination with other ingredients for increased nutrition.

Buttermilk It is traditionally the liquid which remains after the fat is removed from cream during the butter churning process. It's most

often commercially available in a cultured form made from nonfat milk and a small amount (1% or less) of butter. It is somewhat thick and has a pleasant tangy flavor.

Sour milk It is sweet milk made sour by the addition of an acid (see page 18). It is used in baked products leavened with baking soda.

Cream It is the butterfat in cow's milk. Commercial cream varies in butterfat content. Cream must contain at least 25% butterfat to be whipped successfully. Two-day-old cream will whip to a greater volume than fresh cream.

Half-and-half It is a mixture of ½ milk and ½ cream and contains 10% to 20% butterfat.

Light or pastry cream It is cream containing approximately 30% butterfat.

Heavy, or whipping, cream It is cream containing 36% to 40% butterfat.

Sour cream It is artificially soured sweet cream and is very thick and flavorful, containing about 18% butterfat.

Eggs
Because they perform so many

different functions, eggs are the most interesting ingredient in homemade products. They are the only one of our ingredients, with the exception of milk, which is a completely palatable food dish when eaten alone.

In combination with other ingredients they add color, flavor, and a delicate texture to the finished product. In the presence of oven heat, the proteins in egg and the gluten complex of flour coagulate, change from a fluid to a thickened substance, and set the structure of baked products. Other functions of the egg are thickening (pudding), binding (muffins), emulsifying or evenly distributing a fine oily liquid in a second liquid (mayonnaise), clarifying or clearing a liquid of impurities (soup), and leavening (cake).

The color of an eggshell is an inherited characteristic of the chicken that laid it and in no way affects the quality of the egg itself.

Always use the freshest eggs available to you. A fresh egg has a high yolk with a large portion of thick white around it and a small portion of thin white. As the egg ages, the yolk flattens and the white becomes very thin. The yolks of old eggs break very easily.

Fats

Fats tenderize and soften baked products. Baked products containing only small amounts of fats, or no fats at all, tend to dry out very quickly. Fats also add flavor and greatly improve the texture and consistency of all homemade products.

Fats are classified as either solid or liquid depending upon their state at room temperature. It is of utmost importance that you use fat in the form that is called for in a recipe. The characteristic flakiness of biscuits is caused by the large areas of solid fat kneaded into the dough. Muffins, on the other hand, require a liquid or melted fat to combine with the other ingredients to produce the required texture.

Fats are derived from both vegetable and animal sources. The common vegetable fats, usually referred to as salad oils, are obtained from various nuts, seeds, and plant materials. These include the olive, peanut, cottonseed, soybean, and safflower seed. Solid vegetable fat is referred to as shortening. Margarine is a vegetable fat that has been hardened to the consistency of butter by the chemical process of hydrogenation.

The common animal fats include cream, cream cheese, butter, bacon fat, and lard. Animal fat can also be seen as the fine marbling that contributes to both the tenderness and taste of quality meats.

Since butter has by far the

best flavor of all these fats, we strongly recommend its use, whether in solid or melted form, and always call for butter in our recipes except in a few special cases.

Salt and Flavorings

As a flavoring, salt serves two purposes in homemade products. It adds a flavor of its own and enhances the other flavors. However, excessive amounts of salt can make any food quite disagreeable. Too much salt in a yeast bread will not only give it an unpleasant flavor, but will prevent the dough from rising properly.

The other common flavorings are chocolate, vanilla, spices, dried fruits, nuts, seeds, and the grated rinds of citrus fruits. Always use good quality fresh flavorings, because a good flavor is one of the most desired results in homemade products. Use vanilla or other extracts over artificial flavorings. The results will be worth the difference in price. The flavor of all spices will be improved if you buy them whole and grind them just before using.

Storage of Ingredients

Wheat flour All flours should be stored in the refrigerator if possible, except unbleached white flour which is best stored at room temperature.

Sugar Store at room temperature in an airtight container to prevent absorption of moisture. This is especially important for brown sugar.

Yeast Active dry yeast may be stored in the refrigerator indefinitely or at room temperature for 3 or 4 weeks. Keep the packets or bulk yeast free from moisture. Store cake yeast in the refrigerator for no more than 1 week or in the freezer for no more than 6 months. If the cake yeast is crumbly when opened, it is usually good.

Baking soda Store at room temperature.

Baking powder Store in its own container in a cool place with the lid secured. Moisture destroys baking powder. Buy small cans and replace them often.

Eggs Always keep eggs under refrigeration until just before you are ready to use them. Eggs are always stored with the broad end up. Extra whites may be frozen. As a matter of fact, freezing improves the foaming property of egg whites. Buy smaller quantities of eggs more often.

Milk and cream Store in the refrigerator. Never let either milk or cream stand at room temperature for long periods of time. Store powdered milk in a dry place at room temperature.

Fats Store butter and margarine in the refrigerator or in the freezer for longer periods of time. Vegetable shortenings and oils may be stored in a cool, dark place in a covered container. After a shortening or oil has been heated to smoking, it will rapidly become rancid, no matter how it is stored. Avoid buying large containers that will be stored for long periods of time. Buy smaller amounts more frequently.

Spices Store in a cool, dark place in tightly covered containers. Buy small quantities and replace them every 6 months to 1 year.

Measurements

Dry

1 pinch or dash = ⅛ teaspoon	8 tablespoons = ½ cup
3 teaspoons = 1 tablespoon	10 tablespoons + 2 teaspoons = ⅔ cup
4 tablespoons = ¼ cup	
5 tablespoons + 1 teaspoon = ⅓ cup	12 tablespoons = ¾ cup
	16 tablespoons = 1 cup

Liquid

3 teaspoons liquid = 1 tablespoon liquid
1 tablespoon = ½ fluid ounce
1 cup = 8 fluid ounces =
16 tablespoons
2 cups = 1 pint
4 cups = 2 pints = 1 quart
16 cups = 8 pints = 4 quarts =
1 gallon

Pound equivalents

(All are approximate with the exception of butter.)
1 pound eggs = 8 extra large
eggs
1 pound white sugar = 2 cups
1 pound brown sugar = 2⅓ cups
1 pound powdered sugar =
4 cups
1 pound all-purpose flour =
4 cups, sifted once
1 pound cake flour = 5 cups,
sifted once
1 pound butter = 2 cups
1 pound raisins = 3 cups

Other helpful equivalents

1 cup egg whites = 8 extra large
egg whites
1 cup egg yolks = 12 extra large
egg yolks
1 cup whole eggs = 4 extra large
eggs
1 extra large egg = ¼ cup
1 egg yolk = 2 tablespoons
1 egg white = 2 tablespoons
1 ounce butter = 2 tablespoons
or ¼ stick
4 tablespoons butter = ½ stick
6 tablespoons butter = ¾ stick
8 tablespoons butter = 1 stick =
½ cup butter

2 cups butter = 4 sticks =
1 pound butter
1 square unsweetened chocolate
= 1 ounce
3-ounce package cream cheese =
6 tablespoons
8-ounce package cream cheese =
16 tablespoons
½ pound cottage cheese = 1 cup
¼ pound Cheddar or Swiss
cheese = 1 cup grated cheese
½ pint heavy, or whipping, cream
= 1 cup
1 cup heavy cream = 2 cups
whipped cream
1 envelope unflavored gelatin = 1
tablespoon and will gel 2 cups
of liquid. (Always combine
sugar with liquid before measuring liquid.)
1 standard box of berries = approximately 2 cups
1 cup uncooked long grain rice =
3 cups cooked rice
1 cup precooked rice = 2 cups
cooked rice
1 cup brown rice = 4 cups
cooked rice
8 ounces uncooked pasta =
approximately 4 cups
cooked pasta
2 cups dry white beans = 6 cups
cooked beans
2 cups dry kidney beans = 6 cups
cooked beans
3 cups dry lima beans = 7 cups
cooked beans

Can sizes

6 ounces = ¾ cup
8 ounces = 1 cup
10½ ounces = 1¼ cups
13 ounces = 1½ cups
15½ ounces = 1¾ cups
16 ounces = 1 pound = 2 cups

Substitutions

Wheat flour

To improve the nutritional quality of any white flour, measure 2 teaspoons of wheat germ into the bottom of the measuring cup before measuring flour.

1 cup cake flour = ¾ cup + 2 tablespoons all-purpose flour + 2 tablespoons cornstarch

Sugar

1 cup white sugar = 1 cup powdered sugar = 1 cup brown sugar

1 cup honey = 1 cup white, powdered, or brown sugar (Reduce liquid in the recipe ⅓ cup for every cup of honey used. Lower the baking temperature to 350° or the honey flavor will be lost and excessive browning will occur.)

1 cup molasses = 1 cup white, powdered, or brown sugar (Reduce liquid in the recipe ¼ cup and add 1 teaspoon baking soda for every cup of molasses used.)

1¼ cups, maple sugar = 1 cup white, powdered, or brown sugar (Reduce liquid in the recipe ½ cup for each 1¼ cups of maple sugar used.)

Eggs

1 whole egg = the volume of 2 egg yolks

1 whole egg = the volume of 2 egg whites

2 tablespoons dried whole egg powder + 2 tablespoons water = approximately 1 fresh egg (Do not use dried egg in uncooked mixtures or egg foams.)

Yeast

1 cake compressed yeast = 1 packet active dry yeast = 1 tablespoon bulk dry yeast, and will leaven 8 cups of flour slowly or 4 cups of flour quickly

Baking powder

tablespoon baking soda + 2 tablespoons cream of tartar + 1 tablespoon cornstarch = 4 tablespoons double-acting baking powder

¼ teaspoon baking soda + ½ cup sour milk or buttermilk (to replace ½ cup liquid in recipe) = 1 teaspoon baking powder

Milk

1 cup sour milk = 1 tablespoon distilled white vinegar + sweet milk to make 1 cup

1 cup milk = ¼ cup dry milk + water to make 1 cup

1 cup milk = ½ cup evaporated milk + ½ cup water

1 cup whipping cream = 2 cups whipped cream

1 cup heavy cream = whipped white of 1 egg + 1 cup light cream, whipped separately and folded together

Fat

1 cup butter = ⅞ cup lard

Except in flavor, equal amounts of butter and margarine are equal

Flavorings

1 square unsweetened baking chocolate = 3 tablespoons unsweetened powdered cocoa + 1 tablespoon butter

Thickenings

1 tablespoon cornstarch = 2
  tablespoons flour = 4 teaspoons quick-cooking tapioca
  = 3 egg yolks = 4 tablespoons
  browned flour

Pans

A 9-inch round cake pan = an 8 x
  8 inch square cake pan
An 8-inch round pan = a 7 x 7
  inch square cake pan

Kitchen Procedures

Measuring Ingredients

One common cause of cooking failures is inaccurate measurement of ingredients. Learning to measure properly, that is, to use the right equipment and the correct method, can significantly improve your cooking.

The basic ingredients in most recipes can be divided into groups of solid fats, dry ingredients, and liquids for the purpose of learning the techniques of measuring. Unless otherwise specified in the recipe, baking ingredients should be at room temperature.

Solid fats

To measure solid fats such as butter, margarine, and vegetable shortening, we recommend the water displacement method. To use this method you will need a 2-cup glass measuring cup. The principle is very simple to understand. The quantity of fat called for in the recipe is subtracted from 2 cups, and the measuring cup is filled with water to equal the difference. Next, small amounts of fat are added to the water in the measuring cup until the water level rises to exactly 2 cups. For example, if the recipe calls for ⅔ cup vegetable shortening, subtract ⅔ cup from 2 cups, leaving a difference of 1⅓ cups. Fill the glass measuring cup with 1⅓ cups of water and add shortening to the cup until the water level rises to exactly 2 cups. Carefully remove the shortening and discard the water.

Butter and margarine are usually packaged in ¼-pound sticks. Each stick is an exact measurement. However, if a part of a stick is needed, it is most accurate to measure that portion by the water displacement method.

Melted fats are measured as liquids and are included in that section.

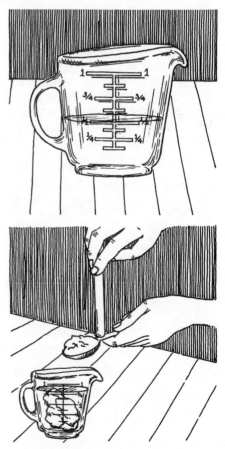

Dry Ingredients

To measure white flour you will need a set of graduated metal measuring cups, a flour sifter, waxed paper, a large spoon, and a knife. Tear off two pieces of waxed paper approximately 12 inches long and place the flour sifter on one of them. Scoop flour into the sifter. You will need to put slightly more flour in the sifter than called for in the recipe. Sift the flour once. Gently lift the sifted flour with a spoon and put it in an appropriately sized metal measuring cup. Fill the measuring cup until it is overflowing. Do not tap, shake, or press the flour into the cup because this destroys the effect of the first sifting. Hold the cup over the waxed paper and make two perpendicular cuts through the flour with a knife to remove any hidden pockets of air. Level off the excess flour with a knife. Place the empty sifter on the clean sheet of waxed paper, pour the flour into it, and sift the flour a second time. Repeat the sifting process as many times as called for in the recipe.

Whole-wheat and rye flours are measured in the same way; they are not sifted.

Sift and measure powdered (confectioners') sugar the same as white flour.

Cornmeal, dry milk, baking powder, baking soda, salt, and spices are not sifted. They are measured directly from the container, using either a metal measuring cup or metal measuring spoons, whichever is appropriate. The excess is always carefully leveled off with a straight-edged knife or spatula.

Granulated sugar is measured in metal measuring cups. Sifting should not be necessary. The excess sugar is leveled off the top of the measuring cup with a knife.

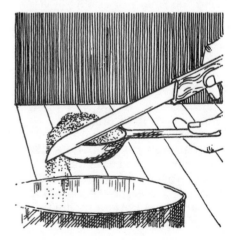

The appropriate sizes of measuring cups should always be used. For example, when you are measuring ¾ cup of sugar, you use a level ½ cup and a level ¼ cup. You never use 1 cup measure and try to eyeball fill it to ¾ cup.

Brown sugar should be packed tightly in the appropriate metal measuring cups and leveled off with a knife. The brown sugar should hold the shape of the cup when it is turned out. If the sugar is lumpy, place the unmeasured sugar between two pieces of waxed paper and crush the lumps with a rolling pin. Discard any remaining lumps.

Liquids

A glass measuring cup is always used to measure liquids, unless the amount to be measured is 1 to 3 tablespoons or less. Metal measuring spoons are used for these small amounts of liquid. Liquid has a tendency to form a meniscus above the top edge of whatever container it is poured into, if the container is filled to the very top with liquid. The meniscus is a mushroom effect in which excess liquid is actually held above the top edge of the container. When you are measuring small amounts of liquid with

measuring spoons, a meniscus can undesirably increase your measurement. Larger quantities of liquid are poured into a glass measuring cup which is resting on a level surface. The measurement is read with the eye at the same level as the liquid to avoid distortion caused by the viewing angle.

Oils, melted fats, and melted chocolate are measured most accurately in a glass measuring cup or a measuring spoon which have first been rinsed in boiling water. The same holds true for honey, syrups, and molasses.

Whipping cream is measured before it is whipped.

Tips for Successful Cooking and Baking

□ Use only high quality ingredients or don't bother starting from scratch. You may as well use the prepared mixes or store-bought varieties.

□ For the safest results never deviate in any way from the recipe and use only recipes from trustworthy sources.

□ Plan your cooking project ahead and read through the recipes thoroughly. Have all ingredients at room temperature except where the recipe indicates otherwise.

□ Before you begin, organize your kitchen. Your job will be many times easier and much more pleasant if everything you need is conveniently laid out. Clear off enough counter space to give yourself ample room to work in. Wash and put away all dirty dishes before you begin to work.

□ Make things easy for yourself. Try to store flour and sugar in a convenient place in canisters or jars with wide openings. French mason jars are well suited to this purpose. They are inexpensive, attractive, and available in a variety of sizes.

□ Measure all ingredients accurately following the procedures on pages 21–23.

□ Remember any shortcomings your oven or burners may have.

□ Never carry on another activity while you are mixing a recipe. Distractions, no matter how small, lead to mistakes.

□ Don't substitute baking soda for baking powder. They are not interchangeable. (See page 12.)

□ When a recipe calls for separated eggs, separate the eggs when you remove them from the refrigerator and then allow them to warm up to room temperature before beating them. Eggs beat to a greater volume when they are at room temperature.

□ Never beat egg whites in a plastic bowl.

□ Don't use a melted fat where a solid fat is specified. Solid and liquid volumes are different.

□ Scrape down the sides of the mixing bowl with a rubber scraper while you are using an electric mixer.

□ Never grease the sides of a cake or quick-bread pan. Grease the bottom only with butter. The batter cannot cling to the slippery sides of a thoroughly greased pan and will not be able to rise as high.

□ Always use the pan size specified in the recipe. Changing the pan size also alters the baking temperature and time. Larger, more shallow pans need increased heat; smaller, deeper pans need decreased heat.

□ Lustrous metal pans give the best distribution of heat for cakes and cookies. Old, blackened pans do not work as

24

well. Glass is best for pies because it holds the heat longer and the pie crust will continue browning after the pie has been removed from the oven. Heavy cast-iron pans work best for muffins and rolls.

□ Don't double or divide recipes. It is better to freeze half the finished product or mix the ingredients together twice.

□ Use a timer every time you bake in the oven.

□ Never increase a cooking temperature because you are in a hurry.

□ Don't open the oven door prematurely. A draft may cause your baked product to fall.

□ Altitudes above 3,000 feet alter ingredient amounts and baking times. Consult your local state university extension service for more exact information related to your area.

Standard Utensil Sizes

The right tools are necessary to do any job correctly. We recommend the following utensils for every well-equipped kitchen:

glass measuring cup, 2-cup volume

set of graduated metal measuring cups, 1, ½, ⅓, ¼ cups

set of graduated metal measuring spoons, 1 tablespoon, 1, ½, ¼ teaspoon

bread bowl, extra large pottery mixing bowl, 15-inch diameter x 7-inch depth

large mixing bowl, 12-inch diameter x 6-inch depth

medium mixing bowl, 9-inch diameter x 5-inch depth

small mixing bowl, 6-inch diameter x 4-inch depth

flour sifter, 3-cup volume

medium saucepan, 2-quart volume

small saucepan, 1-pint volume

jelly kettle, 9- or 10-quart volume

large kettle, 4-quart volume

cooling rack, 12 x 8 inches

bread pans, 9 x 5 inches x 3-inch depth

baking sheet, 17½ x 11½ inches x 1-inch depth

quick bread pan, 12 x 3½ inches x 3½-inch depth

cast-iron muffin pan, wells, 2½-inch diameter

round glass pie pan with sloped sides, 9-inch diameter

round tube cake pan, 9½-inch diameter x 3½-inch depth

round tube cake pan, 8-inch diameter x 3-inch depth

oblong cake pan, 9 x 13 inches x 2-inch depth

round cake pans (two or three will be needed for layer cakes), 9-inch diameter x 2-inch depth

square cake pan, 9 x 9 inches x 2-inch depth

square cake pan, 8 x 8 inches x 2-inch depth

set of graduated biscuit cutters, 1½-, 2-, 2⅜-, 2¾-inch diameters

Yeast-Raised Breads

To make a good loaf of yeast-raised bread requires time, careful attention to detail, and patience, but the rewards are great. We personally would rather bake bread than prepare any other kind of food. For us there is a great deal of personal satisfaction involved in the feel of the dough while kneading, the warmth and smell of the bread while it is baking, and the sight of beautiful golden brown loaves set out to cool. This process never fails to improve our states of mind.

Yeast-raised breads are leavened by a tiny one-celled plant called yeast, which produces carbon dioxide as it ferments. Under favorable conditions the yeast plant will multiply rapidly. To bake a successful yeast bread you must learn to provide the yeast plant with everything it needs. This will not be difficult if you follow our recipes exactly. The recipe for basic white bread describes and illustrates in detail all the general procedures for baking bread.

We have divided yeast-raised breads into three groups: Loaf (table) breads for everyday use, dinner rolls, and sweet breads for special occasions. A knowledge of all of these breads will be sure to increase your reputation as a cook.

Loaf Breads

These are the breads you use every day for toast, sandwiches, and as an accompaniment to any meal. Since they form such an important part of your diet, they should be interesting and pleasing to the taste. We have included a variety of recipes for daily loaf breads. You may wish to find your favorite and bake this one repeatedly, or you may thrive on variety and bake them all in turn. In any case, each of the following recipes will produce a fine loaf of bread.

If you are an experienced bread maker, these instructions will be too detailed for you. However, you may wish to read through them for pointers that may improve your own technique. If your method differs from ours and works well, continue baking bread your way. There is no right or wrong method if the results are satisfactory.

If you are an inexperienced or new bread maker, read these instructions over very carefully before you begin. Also, read the section on proper measuring on pages 21–23. This is extremely important, for measurements which are not exact will produce less than satisfactory results.

Before you begin mixing your bread, set out all the ingredients and utensils on your kitchen counter. Also, plan to spend a minimum of 4 hours at home so you can give the bread the attention it will need through the mixing, kneading, rising, and baking stages. If everything is carefully laid out before you and you follow these instructions exactly, there should be no chance of failure and you will produce beautiful loaves of bread.

Note: All of the following recipes call for packets of active dry yeast because it is the easiest yeast to purchase. The flavor of cake yeast is superior, and if you have a good source for fresh cake yeast, use it. Simply crumble the cake yeast in the warm water and proceed as directed.

Basic White Bread

Quantity: Two loaves
Oven Temperature: 375° F.
Baking Time: Check after 30 minutes

Ingredients

2 packets active dry yeast, recently purchased
½ cup 90° F. water
2 cups milk, whole or low-fat
½ cup butter
¼ cup white sugar
2 teaspoons salt
¼ cup wheat germ (optional)
4 cups unbleached white flour
2½ to 3½ cups additional unbleached white flour

Extra

butter for greasing bowl and baking pans
egg glaze or seeds for top of bread (see Shaping Step 5)

Utensils

glass measuring cup
set of graduated metal measuring cups
set of measuring spoons
bread bowl
flour sifter
electric mixer (optional)
medium saucepan
clean kitchen towel
kitchen thermometer
pastry brush
2 metal bread pans
cooling rack
kitchen timer
hot pad

Procedure

Mixing

1. Read the chapter introduction.
2. Measure out 2 cups of milk in the glass measuring cup and pour it into the saucepan. Set the pan aside for a moment and wash out the measuring cup.
3. Run the tap water to a temperature of 90° F. Check it with your thermometer and fill the clean glass measuring cup with ½ cup of 90° water. Empty both packets of yeast into the water and stir to begin the dissolving process. Set the measuring cup in a warmish, draft-free place. We usually put ours over the pilot light of a gas stove or in a barely warm oven with the door closed.
□ Water cooler than 85° F. will retard the growth of the yeast; water hotter than 110° F. will kill it.
□ Warm the oven by turning it on 200°, or low, for 1 or 2 minutes and then shutting it off.
4. Place the saucepan on the stove and set flame or burner at a low temperature. Stir occasionally until the milk is scalded. (The milk is scalded when a thin skin forms on the surface of the milk and bubbles begin to form around the edges. Do not boil the milk or heat it over a high flame.) Remove the pan from the heat.
□ The scalding process is important because it prevents bacteria in the milk from killing the yeast and also guards against potential souring.
5. Cut the ¼-pound stick of butter into eight to ten pieces. Add them to the scalded milk and stir until they are dissolved. Now add ¼ cup honey or sugar and 2 teaspoons of salt. Stir to dissolve. Pour the mixture into the mixing bowl and cool it to 90°.
□ This process may be hastened by stirring or by placing the entire bowl in a pan of cool water. Don't

overcool the mixture as this will slow the growth of the yeast, which begins in Step 7.

6. Check the yeast and water mixture. All the grains of yeast should be dissolved and turned into a thick, milky, putty-gray substance with bubbles on top. If the yeast mixture does not look like this, discard it and start over again.

□ If the yeast is not a live substance, your bread will not rise and will be instead a dense, heavy, disappointing failure. Before starting the yeast mixture over again, double-check the expiration date on the yeast package. If the date indicates the yeast should still be good, it is advisable to try yeast purchased at another market. Possibly the first packets of yeast were not stored properly. If the failure of the yeast mixture delays your baking for a long period of time, it is a good idea to refrigerate the milk mixture; or for a shorter period of time, place the bowl containing the milk mixture in the oven and close the door. The oven should be turned off.

7. Stir the healthy yeast into the cooled scalded milk mixture. At this point, for added nutrition, add the ¼ cup wheat germ and stir.

8. Sift 4 cups of flour into the bowl, 1 cup at a time, beating with the electric mixer or by hand after every addition.

□ This mixing process is important because it begins to develop the gluten structure, which will eventually hold up the bread, making it light and tender instead of dense and tough.

9. Allow the dough to rest for 10 minutes. This will make it less sticky when you knead it.

10. Set the bowl on a sturdy counter top at a comfortable height for working the dough in the bowl. Sift 1 cup of flour over the top of the dough and begin kneading in the bowl. This is the way to knead: Starting with the edge of dough closest to you, push the dough away from you lightly with the heels of your hands. Now pull the outside edge over the top of the dough. Turn the dough inside the bowl a quarter-turn and repeat the motions. Continue pushing, pulling, and turning the dough in a nice steady rhythm, curving your fingers around the edge of the dough while you work to prevent excessive flattening. This dough has a high proportion of fat and should be relatively easy to knead.

□ Doughs with a low- or no-fat content, like French bread dough, will be more difficult to knead; doughs with a very high fat content, like sweet bread dough, will be easier to knead.

□ Never increase the fat content of your dough for ease in kneading, as this will also inhibit the growth of the gluten structure and the bread will not rise as well.

11. After you have completely worked in the first cup of flour, continue adding flour ½ cup at a time, kneading each flour addition into the dough completely before adding more. You will probably have to discontinue the sifting at this point because of the sticky dough on your hands. We usually scoop the flour from a canister with a measuring cup. Work the dough that is stuck to the sides of the bowl and your hands into the large mass of dough while you work.

□ This is necessary or the separated dough will become coated with flour and make hard lumps on the surface of the dough which never quite disappear.

12. As the dough becomes less sticky you may want to remove it from the bowl to a lightly floured board for the final kneading. Continue kneading and adding small amounts of flour to the dough un-

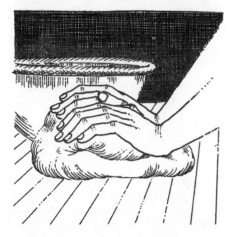

til it is no longer sticky and has a smooth, elastic feel. Air bubbles will begin to form on the surface. You can hear them break as you knead. The amount of flour needed to finish the dough will vary from one batch of bread to

another. Don't worry about adding exact quantities of flour; just keep on sprinkling small (½ cup) amounts of flour on the dough and working them in until the dough achieves the desired smooth, elastic consistency.

□ The kneading process is important as it completes the mixing of the ingredients and further develops the gluten structure of the bread. Normal kneading time for 2 loaves of bread is 12 minutes, but the feel of the dough is more important than actual kneading time.

□ Kneading that is rough instead of even and smooth breaks the gluten strands causing large holes and poor volume.

13. If your mixing bowl feels cold to the touch, warm it by filling the bowl with hot water from the tap. Empty the bowl, dry it well, and lightly grease the entire inside with a tiny amount of the extra butter. Shape the dough into a smooth ball and place it in the bowl with any rough edges on the bottom. If you are planning to let

the dough rise more than once in the bowl, lightly grease the top of the dough as well. (Some bakers let the dough rise more than

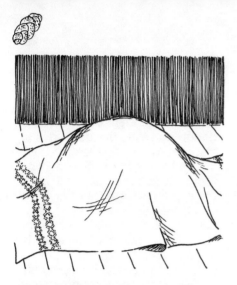

once, depending on when they plan to serve it.) Wet a clean kitchen towel and wring out all of the excess water. The towel should not be drippy. Completely cover the top of the bowl with the towel.

Rising

1. If you have unlimited time to spend close to your kitchen, you may allow the dough to rise at room temperature (68° to 72° F.) in a draft-free place. This process may be helped by placing the bowl of dough on a heating pad set on medium. Check the towel every ½ hour to be sure it is still damp. If the towel dries out, a crust will form on the top of the dough. Or, you may place the dough in a slightly warmed, shut-off oven for approximately 1 hour. Check the dough after ½ hour to be sure the towel is still damp and the oven is warm. The bowl should still be warm to the touch. If the bowl is cold, remove it from the oven and turn the oven on to warm (200°) for 2 or 3 minutes. Turn the oven off and replace the bowl.

2. The dough will have risen enough when blisters of gas begin to appear on top of the dough

and it has doubled in bulk. Press two of your fingers deeply into the dough. If the impression remains, the dough has risen enough.

3. Punch the dough down by

plunging your fist into the center. Fold the edges of the dough over from all four sides and punch it down again. Do this two or three times to break up the large gas pockets which formed while the dough was rising. (If these gas pockets are not broken up they will form large holes in the finished loaves of bread.) Turn the dough over so the smooth side is up.

□ If you are not ready to bake the bread you may allow it to rise another time in the bowl. This should take about 1 hour. Repeat punching down process. You may allow the bread to rise a third time, though this is not necessary. However, as long as you do not allow the surface of the bread to dry out, the extra periods of rising actually improve the texture of the bread.

Shaping

1. Sprinkle your bread board lightly with flour and turn the punched down dough out onto the board. Cut it into two equal

pieces. At this point we usually throw each piece of dough down on the bread board vigorously two or three times to be sure all the gas bubbles are broken up. Round each piece of dough into a ball and place both on the bread board. Cover with a clean towel and allow the dough to rest for 10 minutes. This will make it easier to handle while shaping.

2. While the dough is resting, generously grease the bottom and sides of the 2 bread pans with the extra butter.

□ Do not use oil for this purpose, because the bread dough will absorb the oil and the bread will stick to the pan. Butter is not absorbed by dough in the same way.

3. You may shape the dough into loaves with your hands and place them in the pans with any rough edges on the bottom. Or, for more precisely shaped loaves, follow these steps:

a. With your hands, carefully flatten, without punching or pounding, one of the balls into an oblong.

b. Fold the edge of one of the long sides to the center and press to seal.

c. Fold the second long edge to the center and press to seal.

d. Flatten the dough again slightly and stretch it by pulling gently on both ends until it is twice the length of a bread pan.

e. Bring both ends to the center, overlapping them slightly, and press to seal.

f. Roll the dough gently with your fingers curved around it. This action will seal the edges and round the loaf.

g. Place the shaped dough, seam side down, carefully in a

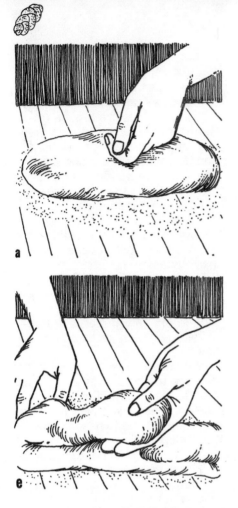

a

b

e

f

pan and gently stretch the ends out to fill the corners of the pan.

h. Repeat with the second ball of dough.

□ It is important to form the loaf of bread properly or the top crust will separate from the rest of the loaf.

4. Place both pans in a warmed shut-off oven for ½ hour or until the dough has almost doubled in bulk.

5. Though it is not a necessity, a glaze will add a beautiful finishing touch to your bread. If you wish to use one, it should be carefully

applied at this time. With a pastry brush, cover the entire top of

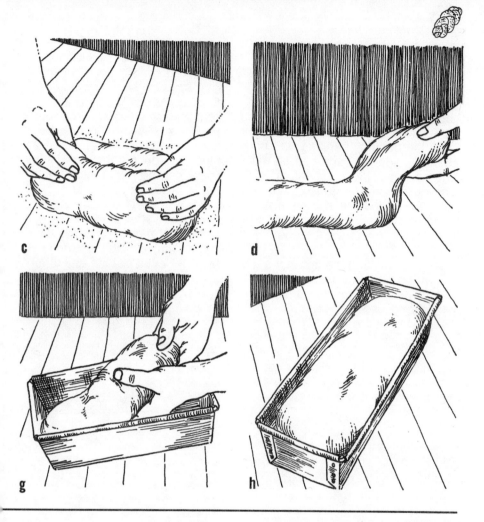

c

d

g

h

each loaf with one of the following glazes. Don't brush too much glaze on your bread or the excess will run down the sides into the pan and cause the bread to stick.

    a. For a rich brown crust: Beat 1 egg yolk with 1 or 2 tablespoons of water.

    b. For a normal crust: Beat 1 whole egg with 1 or 2 tablespoons of water.

    c. For a shiny crust: Beat 1 egg white with 1 or 2 tablespoons of water.

    d. If you like a seeded crust, sprinkle (don't pour) poppy or sesame seeds generously and

evenly over the top of a loaf that has been coated with Glaze c.

6. Return bread pans to the oven, placing them 2 inches apart in the center of the middle rack position. Set the oven temperature to 375° and the timer for 30 minutes. Check the bread when the timer goes off. If the tops are browning too fast (they have turned a dark golden brown at this stage of baking), turn the oven down 25° and cover the top of each loaf with aluminum foil. The foil slows down the browning process. Set the timer for another 10 minutes and check the bread again when the timer goes off. It should have a rich golden brown crust which gives a hollow sound when tapped with your knuckles.

7. Remove the bread immediately from the pans by banging one of the long sides of each pan on the counter top. The bread should pop out easily. If it doesn't, carefully loosen the bread from the sides of the pan with a knife and bang the pan against the counter again.

□ If the loaf still does not come out of the pan, you must pull it out with your hands. (This happened because you did not grease the pan properly.)

8. Brush the tops of your loaves, using a pastry brush, with a little melted butter, if you did not apply a glaze before baking. The butter will soften the crust and give it a slight shine.

9. Place the loaves, right side up, on the rack and allow them to cool for several hours. Do not cover the bread while it is cooling or it will become soggy.

10. In our opinion the flavor of

the bread improves as it cools, but if you can't resist sampling a slice of hot, steaming bread, please cut your bread in this way. Heat a serrated knife with a blade of at least 10 inches over the stove burner or flame for 1 or 2 minutes. Now cut the bread with a gentle sawing motion and firm but gentle pressure on the knife.

□ Hot bread will squash and tear if you cut it with a cold knife.

□ Invest in a good bread knife with an ample blade, as bread does not cut well with any other kind of knife.

11. When the bread has cooled to room temperature, wrap it in plastic bags, remove all excess air, and seal. You may freeze one of the loaves to maintain freshness. To defrost a frozen loaf of bread, remove it from the freezer, take it out of the plastic bag, and rewrap it in aluminum foil. Place the bread immediately in a 300° oven for 30 minutes. Cool. This method will prevent any sogginess from moisture in the freezer and will give you a nearly fresh baked loaf of bread.

French Bread

Quantity: One large loaf, or two
  small loaves
Oven Temperature: 400° F.
Baking Time: Check after 30 minutes

Ingredients

1 packet active dry yeast
1½ cups 90° F. water
2 teaspoons salt
1 tablespoon white sugar
3 cups unbleached white flour
1 to 2 cups additional unbleached white flour

Extra

butter to grease bowl and baking
  sheet
white cornmeal
1 egg white for glaze

Special utensils

baking sheet
oven rack covered with ceramic
  tiles
pan of boiling water

Procedure

Mixing

1. Read through the directions for
Basic White Bread.
2. Run the tap water to a temperature of 90° F. Check it with your
thermometer and fill the clean
glass measuring cup with 1½
cups of 90° water. Empty the
yeast packet into the water and
stir to begin the dissolving process. Set the measuring cup in a
warmish draft-free place.
3. Sift the 2 teaspoons of salt, 1
tablespoon of white sugar, and 3
cups of flour together.
4. After the yeast mixture has
bubbled up in the measuring cup,
place it in a large mixing bowl.

□ To hasten the rising process,
you may warm the bowl in a 200°
oven or with hot tap water.
5. Slowly add the flour mixture,
beating it in with an electric
mixer. This will begin to develop
the gluten structure and make the
bread easier to knead.
6. Clean the dough from the beaters and continue instructions for
Basic White Bread beginning with
Mixing Step 9.

Shaping

1. Shape the dough into 1 large
loaf or divide it into 2 small loaves
following the instructions for
shaping Basic White Bread. Place
the shaped loaves on a greased
baking sheet that has been sprinkled with white cornmeal. If you
make 2 small loaves, leave space
on the baking sheet between the
loaves. The bread will double in
size during rising.
2. Place the bread in a warmed,
shut-off oven for ½ hour or until
the dough has almost doubled in
bulk.
□ Watch this dough carefully.
Bread that rises on a baking sheet
will collapse if allowed to rise too
long.
3. Put a kettle of water on to boil.
4. After the bread has risen,
brush the entire exposed surface
of the bread with a glaze made
from 1 egg white beaten with 1 or
2 tablespoons of water.
5. Place a pan of boiling water on
the floor of the oven, and if you
have them, place the tiles on the
lower rack. Now position the
bread on the top rack and set
your timer for 30 minutes. When
the timer goes off, brush the

bread one more time with the egg white glaze and return it to the oven to finish baking.

6. When the bread is done, remove it from the baking sheet to a rack to cool.

□ French bread is best eaten fresh.

Shaker Daily Loaf

Quantity: One large loaf
Oven Temperature: 375°
Baking Time: Check after 30 minutes

Ingredients
   1 packet active dry yeast
  ¼ cup 90° F. water
   2 cups milk
   2 tablespoons butter
   2 tablespoons white sugar
   2 teaspoons salt
   4 cups unbleached white flour
1½ to 2 cups additional unbleached white flour

Extra
butter for greasing bowl and baking pan

Procedure
Follow the directions for Basic White Bread.

Garlic and Onion Bread

Quantity: Two medium loaves
Oven Temperature: 400° F.
Baking Time: Check after 30 minutes

Ingredients
- 2 packets active dry yeast
- 2 cups 90° F. water
- 2 medium onions
- 2 cloves garlic
- ¼ cup olive oil
- ¼ cup finely chopped parsley (optional)
- 2 teaspoons dried basil or 4 teaspoons finely chopped fresh basil (optional)
- 2 teaspoons salt
- 1 tablespoon white sugar
- 4 cups unbleached white flour
- 3 to 4 cups additional unbleached white flour

Extra
butter to grease bowl and baking sheet
white cornmeal
1 egg white for glaze

Special utensils
baking sheet
oven rack covered with ceramic tiles
pan of boiling water

Procedure
1. Read through the directions for Basic White Bread and French Bread.
2. Chop the onions and garlic very fine with a sharp French knife. Sauté them in the frying pan at a low heat in the ¼ cup olive oil until they are transparent but not brown.
□ Do not walk away and leave the onion and garlic mixture on the heat. It will burn easily.
3. Cool the onion-garlic mixture to lukewarm. Stirring will hasten the cooling process. Add the optional parsley or basil and put the mixture in a large mixing bowl.
4. Follow the directions given for French Bread, adding the yeast and water to the onion-garlic mixture in the large mixing bowl.

Dill Rye Bread

Quantity: Two round loaves
Oven Temperature: 400° F.
Baking Time: Check after 30 minutes

Ingredients

2 packets active dry yeast
2 cups 90° F. water
½ cup butter
2 tablespoons white sugar
2 teaspoons salt
2 tablespoons dill weed
2 tablespoons dill or caraway seed
2 cups rye flour
3½ to 4 cups white unbleached flour

Extra

butter to grease bowl and baking sheet
yellow cornmeal
1 whole egg for glaze

Special utensils

baking sheet
oven rack covered with ceramic tiles
pan of boiling water

Procedure

1. Read through the directions for Basic White Bread and follow them, adding the dill weed and dill or caraway seed to the liquid ingredients just before you begin adding flour. Add all the rye flour first.

2. At the shaping step, divide the dough in two and shape each half into a small round loaf. Place the loaves on a greased baking sheet that has been sprinkled with yellow cornmeal. Leave space between the loaves to allow for rising.

3. Place the bread in a warmed, shut-off oven for ½ hour or until the dough has almost doubled in bulk.

□ Watch this dough carefully. Bread that rises on a baking sheet will collapse if allowed to rise too long.

4. Put a kettle of water on to boil.

5. Before baking, brush the bread with a glaze made from 1 whole egg beaten with 1 or 2 tablespoons of water.

6. Place a pan of boiling water on the floor of the oven, and if you have them, place the tiles on the lower rack. Now position the bread on the top rack and bake it.

7. Set your timer for 30 minutes when the bread begins to bake. When the timer goes off, brush the bread one more time with the egg glaze and return it to the oven to finish baking.

8. When the bread is done, remove it from the baking sheet to a rack to cool.

□ This bread is best eaten fresh.

Cheese Bread

Quantity: Two loaves
Oven Temperature: 375° F.
Baking Time: Check after 30 minutes

Ingredients
2 packets active dry yeast
1 cup 90° F. water
¼ cup butter
1 tablespoon white sugar
1½ teaspoons salt
1 cup mashed potato (no extra butter added)
2 cups grated Jarlsberg or Jack cheese
4 extra large eggs
4 cups unbleached white flour
2½ to 3½ cups additional unbleached white flour

Extra
butter for greasing bowl and baking pans
egg glaze (optional)
sesame seeds for top (optional)

Procedure
1. Read through the directions for Basic White Bread.
2. Boil 2 medium-size potatoes until they are soft. Drain off all but 1 or 2 tablespoons of water and beat the potatoes until they are smooth with your electric mixer. Measure out 1 level cup of mashed potatoes in a metal measuring cup and scrape the potatoes into a large mixing bowl. Or, reconstitute 1 cup of instant mashed potatoes using no butter or salt.
3. Grate the cheese and measure out 2 cups. Place cheese in the bowl with the mashed potatoes.
4. Beat the eggs enough to mix them together completely. This can be easily done in a small bowl with a fork. Add the eggs to the cheese and potato mixture. If the potatoes are still steaming hot, add a small amount of the potato and cheese mixture to the eggs before adding the eggs to the potato-cheese mixture. This will raise the temperature of the eggs and prevent them from cooking when they are added to the hot potato mixture.
5. Proceed following the directions (not the ingredients list) for Basic White Bread, adding the yeast and water to the potato-cheese-egg mixture in the large mixing bowl.

Mary Thorne-Thomsen's Bread

Quantity: Four loaves
Oven Temperature: 375° F.
Baking Time: Check after 30 minutes

Ingredients

3 packets active dry yeast
½ cup 90° F. water
1 quart buttermilk
1 cup butter
¾ cup honey
4 teaspoons salt
¾ cup wheat germ
¼ cup soy flour
½ cup powdered skim milk
2 cups mashed potatoes (no extra butter added)
8 cups unbleached white flour
4 to 5 cups additional unbleached white flour

Extra

butter for greasing bowl and baking pans
egg glaze for top (optional)

Procedure

1. Read through the directions for Basic White Bread.
2. Boil 4 medium-size potatoes until they are soft. Drain off all but 1 or 2 tablespoons of water and beat the potatoes until they are smooth with your electric mixer. Measure out 2 level cups of mashed potatoes in a metal measuring cup and scrape the potatoes into an extra large mixing bowl. Or, reconstitute 2 cups of instant potatoes using no butter or salt.
3. Add ¾ cup honey, ¾ cup wheat germ, ¼ cup soy flour, and ½ cup powdered skim milk to the mashed potatoes.
4. Proceed following directions for Basic White Bread, adding the yeast and water to the potato mixture in the large mixing bowl.

Honey Whole-Wheat Bread

Quantity: Two loaves
Oven Temperature: 375° F.
Baking Time: Check after 30 minutes

Ingredients

2 packets active dry yeast
½ cup 90° F. water
1½ cups milk
½ cup butter
¾ cup honey
2 teaspoons salt
½ cup wheat germ (optional)
3 cups whole-wheat flour
2 cups unbleached white flour
1 to 2 cups additional unbleached white flour

Extra

butter to grease bowl and baking pans
1 egg for glaze
sesame seeds

Procedure

Follow the directions for Basic White Bread. Add the whole-wheat flour before adding white flour.

Anadama Bread

Quantity: Two loaves
Oven Temperature: 375° F.
Baking Time: Check after 30 minutes

Ingredients

2 packets active dry yeast
½ cup 90° F. water
¾ cup milk
¼ cup butter
1 cup boiling water
¾ cup yellow cornmeal
½ cup light molasses
1 extra large egg
2 teaspoons salt
4 cups unbleached white flour
2 to 3 cups additional unbleached white flour

Extra

butter to grease bowl and baking pans

Procedure

1. Read through the directions for Basic White Bread.
2. Bring a tea kettle of water to boil. Measure out 1 cup of boiling water in a glass measuring cup.
3. Measure out ¾ cup yellow cornmeal in metal measuring cup and turn into a large mixing bowl. Pour the 1 cup of boiling water over the cornmeal and stir.
4. Rinse the glass measuring cup in boiling water and measure out ½ cup of molasses. Add this to the cornmeal mixture.
5. Beat the egg in a small bowl with a fork and carefully add it to the cornmeal and molasses mixture. Be sure the mixture has cooled to lukewarm or it will cook the egg.
6. Proceed following directions for Basic White Bread, adding the yeast and water to the cornmeal mixture in the large mixing bowl.

Oatmeal Bread

Quantity: Two medium loaves
Oven Temperature: 375° F.
Baking Time: Check after 30 minutes

Ingredients

2 packets active dry yeast
½ cup 90° F. water
1½ cups milk
¼ cup butter
¼ cup light molasses or honey
2 teaspoons salt
1 extra large egg
1 cup uncooked oatmeal
3½ cups unbleached white flour
1½ to 2½ cups additional unbleached white flour

Extra

butter to grease bowl and baking pans

Procedure

Follow the directions for Basic White Bread. Lightly beat the egg and combine it with the scalded milk, melted butter, and honey. Add the uncooked oatmeal to this mixture before adding the flour.

Dinner Rolls

Freshly baked, piping hot dinner rolls add a special touch to any dinner. If you have several hours free to devote to dinner, you might like to try one of these recipes.

Dough prepared for use as dinner rolls is mixed following the same basic procedures used for loaf breads. There is one important difference. Because it contains less flour than bread dough, roll dough is softer. Most of the kneading may be done with a heavy-duty electric mixer.

Shaping is the most interesting part of making dinner rolls. Simple round rolls may be baked side by side in rectangles, squares, or circles, depending on the shape of the pan. Or, the dough may be formed into Parker House, cloverleaf, crescent, fan-tan, and twist shapes. The tops can be plain, glazed, or sprinkled with seeds. In short, the same dough may take on any number of interesting and very different appearances.

Shaped Dinner Rolls

Quantity: *Ten medium rolls*
Oven Temperature: *375° F.*
Baking Time: *Check after 20 minutes*

Ingredients
1 packet active dry yeast
½ cup 90° F. water
½ cup milk
2 tablespoons butter
1 tablespoon white sugar
¾ teaspoon salt.
2¼ to 2½ cups unbleached white flour
extra cooking oil

Utensils
glass measuring cup
set of graduated metal measuring cups
set of measuring spoons
medium bowl
flour sifter
electric mixer
small saucepan
clean kitchen towel
pastry brush
kitchen thermometer
baking sheet or muffin pan
kitchen timer
cooling rack
hot pad

Procedure

Mixing
1. Read the chapter introduction.
2. Measure out ½ cup of milk in the glass measuring cup and pour it into the saucepan. Set the pan aside for a moment and wash out the measuring cup.
3. Run the tap water to a temperature of 90° F. Check it with your thermometer and fill the clean glass measuring cup with ½ cup of 90° water. Empty the packet of yeast into the water and stir to begin the dissolving process. Set the measuring cup in a warmish draft-free place. We usually put ours over the pilot light of a gas

stove or in a barely warm oven with the door closed.

☐ Water cooler than 85° F. will retard the growth of the yeast; water hotter than 110° F. will kill it.

☐ Warm the oven by turning it on 200°, or low, for 1 or 2 minutes and then shutting it off.

4. Place the saucepan on the stove and set flame or burner at a low temperature. Stir occasionally until milk is scalded. (The milk is scalded when a thin skin forms on the surface of the milk and bubbles begin to form around the edges. Do not boil the milk or heat it over a high flame.) Remove the pan from the heat.

☐ The scalding process is important because it will prevent the bacteria in the milk from killing the yeast and will also guard against souring.

5. Add the butter to the scalded milk and stir until it is dissolved. Now add the sugar and salt. Stir to dissolve. Pour the mixture into the mixing bowl and cool it to 90°.

6. Check the yeast and water mixture. All the grains of yeast should be dissolved and turned into a thick, milky, putty-gray substance with bubbles on top. If the yeast mixture does not look like this, discard it and start over again.

☐ If the yeast is not alive, your rolls will not rise.

7. Stir the healthy yeast into the scalded milk mixture.

8. Sift 1½ cups of flour into the bowl, ½ cup at a time, beating with the electric mixer after every addition.

☐ This mixing process is important because it begins to develop the gluten structure, which will eventually hold up the bread,

making it light and tender instead of dense and tough.

9. Allow the dough to rest for 10 minutes. This will make it less sticky when you knead it.

10. Set the bowl on a sturdy counter top at a comfortable height for working the dough in the bowl. Sprinkle ½ cup of flour over the top of the dough and begin kneading in the bowl. This dough will be very sticky. This is the way to knead: Starting with the edge of dough closest to you, push the dough away from you, lightly with the heels of your hands. Now pull the outside edge over the top of the dough. Turn the dough inside the bowl a quarter-turn and repeat the process using a gentle rocking motion. Continue pushing and turning the dough in a nice steady rhythm, curving your fingers around the edge of the dough while you work to prevent excessive flattening.

11. After you have completely worked in the first ½ cup of flour, and another ½ cup flour, ¼ cup at a time, kneading each flour addition into the dough completely before adding more. Continue kneading the dough until it has a smooth, elastic feel. Air bubbles will begin to form on the surface. You can hear them break as you knead.

☐ The kneading process is important as it completes the mixing of the ingredients and further develops the gluten structure of the bread.

☐ Kneading that is rough instead of even and smooth breaks the gluten strands, causing large holes and poor volume.

12. Lightly grease the inside of the empty bowl with a tiny amount of the extra butter. Shape the dough into a smooth ball and place it in the center of the bowl with any rough edges on the bottom. Wet a clean kitchen towel and wring out all of the excess water. The towel should not be drippy. Completely cover the top of the bowl with the towel.

Rising

1. If you have unlimited time to spend close to your kitchen, you may allow the dough to rise at room temperature (68° to 72° F.) in a draft-free place. This process may be helped by placing the bowl of dough on a heating pad set on medium. Check the towel every ½ hour to be sure it is still damp. If the towel dries out, a crust will form on the top of the dough. Or, you may place the dough in a slightly warmed, shut-off oven for approximately 1 hour. Check the dough after ½ hour to be sure the towel is still damp and the oven is warm. The bowl should still be warm to the touch. If the bowl is cold, remove it from the oven and turn the oven on to warm (200°) for 2 or 3 minutes. Turn the oven off and replace the bowl.
2. The dough will have risen enough when blisters of gas begin to appear on top of the dough and it has doubled in bulk. Press two of your fingers deeply into the dough; if the impression remains, the dough has risen enough.
3. Punch the dough down by plunging your fist into the center. Fold the edges of the dough over from all four sides and punch down again. Do this two or three times to break up the large gas pockets that formed while the dough was rising. If these gas pockets are not broken up, they will form large holes in the finished loaves of bread. Turn the

dough over so the smooth side is up. Allow the dough to rest for 10 minutes.

Shaping

Cloverleaf rolls
1. Grease each well of a muffin pan with butter.
2. Rub a very small amount of cooking oil over your working surface. Place the dough on the surface and work it into a long, even sausage shape. With a sharp knife cut the dough into equal pieces.

Determine the size of the pieces by experimenting with the first piece or two. Each piece of dough should make a ball the size of a large walnut when shaped in your hands. Shape each piece of dough into a ball.
□ If the dough sticks to your hands, rub a very small amount of salad oil on your hands.
3. Place three balls in each well of the muffin pan. Put the muffin pan in a warmed, shut-off oven for ½ hour or until the dough has doubled in bulk.
□ Fill any empty wells in the muffin pan with an inch of water.
4. Turn the oven on to 375° and set your timer for 20 minutes.

Check the rolls when the timer goes off. Leave the rolls in the oven until they are medium golden brown. Take the rolls out of the oven and allow them to cool for 1 or 2 minutes in the pan. Remove them to a cooling rack and cover with a cloth to keep the rolls warm until you are ready to serve them.

□ Overbaked rolls are very dry and tough.

Parker House rolls

To make Parker House rolls you will need a biscuit cutter or round glass and a rolling pin.

1. Grease a baking sheet with butter.

2. Rub a very small amount of cooking oil over your working surface. Place the dough on the surface and roll it out with a rolling pin to a thickness of ½ inch. Cut the dough with a lightly floured 2-inch-diameter biscuit cutter or glass. Make an indentation through the center of each circle of dough with the dull side of a knife blade. Fold each circle of dough in half over the indentation and place it on the baking sheet with 2 inches clear space in all directions.

□ You may bake the remaining scraps of dough in any shape you wish.

3. Place the baking sheet in a warmed, shut-off oven for ½ hour or until the dough has doubled in bulk.

4. Turn the oven on to 375° and set your timer for 20 minutes. Check the rolls when the timer goes off. Leave the rolls in the oven until they are medium golden brown. Take the rolls out of the oven and allow them to cool for 1 or 2 minutes on the sheet. Remove them to a cooling rack and cover with a cloth to keep the rolls warm until you are ready to serve them.

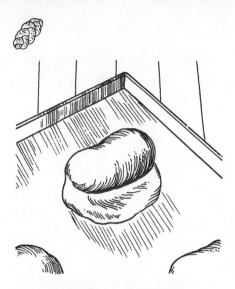

□ Overbaked rolls are very dry and tough.

Fan-tan rolls
To make Fan-tan rolls you will need a rolling pin.
1. Grease each well of a muffin pan with butter.
2. Rub a very small amount of cooking oil over your working surface. Place the dough on the surface and roll it out with a rolling pin to an even thickness of ½ inch. The rolled-out dough should be coaxed into an oblong shape 9 x 16 inches. Cut the oblong shape into fine strips, approximately 1¾ x 16 inches. Melt 1 to

2 tablespoons butter in a small saucepan and lightly brush the top of one strip with butter. Lay a second strip over the first strip and lightly brush the top of the second strip with butter. Continue layering the dough. Don't brush the top of the last layer with butter. Cut the layered dough, perpendicularly to the 16-inch length, into ten equal pieces.
3. Place a piece of layered dough in each well of a muffin pan. Place the pan in a warmed, shut-off oven for ½ hour or until the dough has doubled in bulk.
□ Fill any empty wells in the muffin pan with an inch of water.

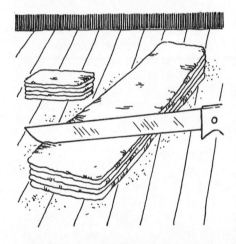

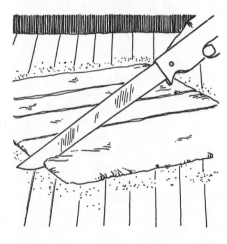

4. Turn the oven on to 375° and set your timer for 20 minutes. Check the rolls when the timer goes off. Leave the rolls in the oven until they are medium golden brown. Take the rolls out of the oven and allow them to cool for 1 or 2 minutes in the pan. Remove them to a cooling rack and cover with a cloth to keep the rolls warm until you are ready to serve them.

□ Overbaked rolls are very dry and tough.

Crescent rolls
To make crescent rolls you will need a rolling pin and a sharp knife.

1. Grease a baking sheet with butter.

2. Rub a very small amount of cooking oil over your working surface. Place the dough on the surface and roll it out with a rolling pin in a circular shape to a thickness of ½ inch. Cut the dough with a sharp knife into four quarters. Cut each quarter into four equal pie-shaped pieces.

3. Melt 1 to 2 tablespoons of butter in a small saucepan. Lightly brush the top of the dough with butter. Shape each crescent roll starting at the outside edge of the circle of dough and rolling one cut-out section of dough toward the center. Place each rolled-up piece on the baking sheet with 2 inches clear space in all directions.

4. Place the baking sheet in a warmed, shut-off oven for ½ hour or until the dough has doubled in bulk. Turn the oven on to 375° and set your timer for 20 minutes. Check the rolls when the timer goes off. Leave the rolls in the oven until they are medium golden brown. Take the rolls out

of the oven and allow them to cool for 1 or 2 minutes in the pan. Remove them to a cooling rack

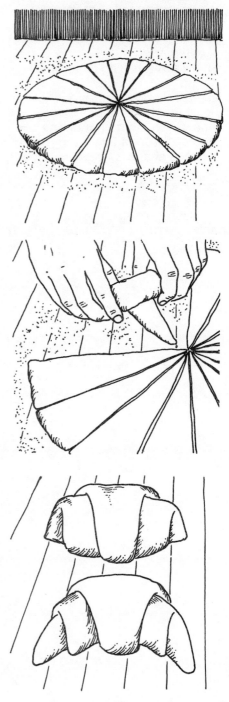

and cover with a cloth to keep the rolls warm until you are ready to serve them.

□ Overbaked rolls are very dry and tough.

Twisted rolls

1. Grease a baking sheet with butter.

2. Rub a very small amount of cooking oil over your working surface. Place the dough on the surface and work it into a long, even sausage shape. Cut the sausage

shape into ten equal pieces. Roll each piece of dough into a long cigar shape. Each piece should be 10 inches long and about ½ inch in diameter.

□ If the dough sticks to your hands, rub a very small amount of salad oil on your hands.

3. Shape each length of dough into a pretzel or knot shape and place each twist of dough on the baking sheet with 2 inches clear space in all directions.

4. Place the baking sheet in a warmed, shut-off oven for ½ hour or until the dough has doubled in bulk. Turn the oven on to 375° and set your timer for 20 minutes. Check the rolls when the timer goes off. Leave the rolls in the oven until they are medium golden brown. Take the rolls out of the oven and allow them to cool for 1 or 2 minutes in the pan. Remove them to a cooling rack and cover with a cloth to keep the rolls warm until you are ready to serve them.

□ Overbaked rolls are very dry and tough.

Refrigerator Potato Rolls

Quantity: Two dozen medium rolls
Oven Temperature: 375° F.
Baking Time: 25 to 30 minutes

Ingredients

1 packet active dry yeast
½ cup 90° F. water
1 cup potato water
½ cup butter
½ cup white sugar
1½ teaspoons salt
1 cup mashed potato
2 extra large eggs
5 to 6 cups unbleached white
   flour

Extra

1 egg white for glaze

Procedure

1. Read the directions for Shaped Dinner Rolls.
2. Boil 2 medium-size potatoes until they are soft. Drain off all but 1 or 2 tablespoons of water and beat the potatoes until they are smooth with your electric mixer. Measure out 1 level cup of mashed potatoes in a metal measuring cup and scrape the potatoes into a large mixing bowl. Or, reconstitute 1 cup of instant mashed potatoes using no butter or salt.
3. Beat the eggs enough to mix them together completely. This can be easily done in a small bowl with a fork. Add the eggs to the mashed potatoes. If the potatoes are still steaming hot, add a small amount of the potatoes to

the eggs. This will raise the temperature of the eggs and prevent them from cooking when they are added to the hot potato mixture.
4. Follow the directions for Shaped Dinner Rolls to Mixing Step 8. Add the potato and egg mixture to the ingredients in the mixing bowl.
5. Add 4 cups of flour to the dough, ½ cup at a time, beating each flour addition in with the electric mixer set at a slow speed. Scrape the dough from the beaters and work in 1-2 cups of flour with your hands. The dough will be very sticky. Grease the sides of the bowl (without removing the dough), cover it with a damp towel, and let the dough rise in a warm place for about 1 hour. Punch the dough down with your fist after it has doubled in bulk and let it stand for 10 minutes. Grease the wells of a muffin tin and fill each well half full of dough. Place the muffin tin in a warmed, shut-off oven to rise. Let them rise until they have doubled in size. Brush the tops of the rolls with a glaze made from beating 1 egg white with 1 to 2 tablespoons water. Bake the rolls, checking them after 20 minutes.
6. The dough may be stored in the refrigerator for up to 5 days. Punch the dough down each day and make sure it is well covered with a damp cloth or piece of waxed paper. Use the dough daily as needed.

French Dinner Rolls

Quantity: Ten 2 x 3 inch rolls
Oven Temperature: 375° F.
Baking Time: 20 minutes

Ingredients

1 packet active dry yeast
¼ cup 90° F. water
¾ cup lukewarm water
2 tablespoons olive oil
1 tablespoon white sugar
1½ teaspoons salt
2 extra large egg whites
4 cups unbleached white flour

Extra

white cornmeal
1 egg white for glaze
butter for greasing baking sheet

Special utensils

oven rack covered with ceramic
   tiles
pan of boiling water

Procedure

1. Read through the directions for Shaped Dinner Rolls to Shaping.
2. Run the tap water to a temperature of 90° F. Check it with your thermometer and fill the clean glass measuring cup with ¼ cup of 90° water. Empty the yeast packet into the water and stir to begin the dissolving process. Set the measuring cup in a warmish, draft-free place.
3. Sift the white sugar, salt, and 2 cups of flour together. Separate the egg whites from the yolks. Refrigerate the yolks.
4. After the yeast mixture has bubbled up in the measuring cup, place it in a large mixing bowl.

Stir in the egg whites, olive oil, and ¾ cup water.
□ To hasten the rising process, you may warm the empty bowl with hot tap water.
5. Slowly add the flour mixture, beating it in with an electric mixer. This will begin to develop the gluten structure and make the bread easier to knead. Clean the dough from the beaters; knead the bread, working in the additional flour, and allow it to rise as directed in Shaped Dinner Rolls.
6. Shape the rolls like miniature loaves of French bread, 2 x 3 inches. Place them on a greased baking sheet that has been sprinkled with white cornmeal. There should be 3 inches clear space around each roll in all directions.
7. Place the baking sheet in a warmed, shut-off oven for ½ hour or until the dough has almost doubled in bulk.
8. Put a kettle of water on to boil.
9. After the rolls have risen, brush the entire exposed surface of the bread with a glaze made from 1 egg white beaten with 1 to 2 tablespoons of water.
10. Place a pan of boiling water on the floor of the oven, and if you have them, place the tiles on the lower rack. Now position the bread on the top rack and set your timer for 12 minutes. When the timer goes off, brush the rolls one more time with the egg white glaze and return them to the oven to finish baking.
11. When the rolls are done, remove them to a rack to cool. Serve warm.

Sweet and Sticky Rolls

Quantity: *Two and one-half dozen rolls*
Oven Temperature: *350° F.*
Baking Time: *Check after 20 minutes*

Ingredients

Dough
1 packet active dry yeast
¼ cup 90° F. water
1 cup milk
¼ cup butter
⅓ cup brown sugar
1 teaspoon salt
2 extra large egg yolks
grated rind of 1 medium orange
3½ cups unbleached white flour

Filling
8 tablespoons cold butter
1½ cups brown sugar
2 teaspoons cinnamon
½ teaspoon nutmeg
2 cups chopped pecans

Extra

butter to grease bowl and baking sheet
1 extra large egg for glaze (optional)
1 to 2 tablespoons hot water
1 tablespoon corn syrup

Special utensils

2 muffin pans or
  1 large cake pan
rolling pin
pastry brush

Procedure

Mixing and rising

Dough
Follow the directions for Shaped Dinner Rolls to Shaping. Beat the egg yolks with a fork until they are a uniform color and add them to the cooled liquid ingredients. Add the grated orange peel with the egg yolk. While the dough is rising, prepare the filling.

Filling
Measure out all the ingredients except the butter and put them into a mixing bowl. Cut the butter into small pieces, and using your fingers, combine it with the ingredients in the bowl.

Shaping

1. Grease the muffin pans or cake pan with butter.
2. Divide the filling into 2 equal parts. Reserve half for Step 3 and place half in a small saucepan. Add 2 tablespoons of hot water and 1 tablespoon of corn syrup to the filling in the saucepan and heat it over a low flame until it has the consistency of syrup. Spread this syrup around the bottom of the cake pan or divide it evenly among the wells in the greased muffin pan.
3. Rub a very small amount of cooking oil over your work surface. Place the dough on the surface and roll it out with a rolling pin to an oblong shape of 10 x 28 inches and ¼ inch thick. Spread the rolled-out dough with the reserved filling. Beginning with the edge of the dough close to you, roll the dough away from you to form a log. Press to seal the edge.
4. Cut across the log-shaped dough making slices 1-inch thick. Place one slice in each well of the muffin pan or arrange the slices so they just touch in the cake pan. Bake any extra dough in a small pan.

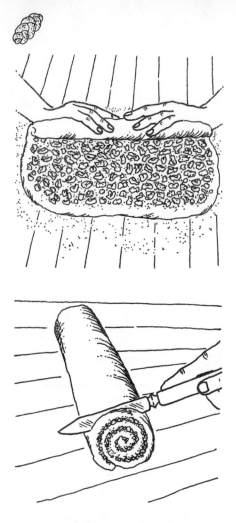

brush, glaze the tops of the rolls with a beaten whole egg.

6. Turn the oven on to 350°. Put the rolls in the oven and set your timer for 20 minutes. If the rolls are baked in the cake pan, allow a little more time.

□ Watch these rolls carefully because the sugar in the filling has a tendency to caramelize and burn.

7. Bake the rolls until they are golden. Remove the rolls from the oven and allow them to cool for 10 minutes before attempting to remove them from the pan. This cooling time will give the filling a chance to become firm. Serve warm.

5. Place the pans in a warmed, shut-off oven and allow the rolls to rise for 30 minutes or until they are double in size. With a pastry

Sweet Breads

Sweet breads follow the same basic mixing procedure used for loaf or table breads. The dough is richer, containing a larger quantity of sugar and butter, less salt and usually at least 2 eggs. The higher proportion of fat makes the sweet dough much easier to knead, because the gluten molecules in the dough slip and slide over each other. When the dough contains too much fat, the bread cannot rise, even though the yeast is doing its proper job. This is because the gluten structure will continually collapse. Don't try to improve a sweet dough by using more butter or by substituting rich milk or cream for regular milk. These both contain a higher percentage of butterfat.

We usually think of this group of sweet yeast-raised breads as ceremonial breads. Many recipes have been handed down through generations, because it is traditional to bake these breads in celebration of a religious or national holiday. You will probably not want to bake them for daily use and will instead make them for special occasions. They may be baked in loaves, braided or twisted, or shaped into any free form that suits your fancy. Bake them plain, frost and decorate them, or fill them with fruit or nuts. Any of the following dough recipes will combine successfully with any of the fillings, glazes, or frostings. Create your own special combination.

Make sweet bread dough almost as stiff as loaf bread dough or it won't hold its shape while it is baking.

Shape your sweet bread in any of the illustrated ways. Use the filling and frosting of your choice.

Basic Sweet Bread

Quantity: One large free-form loaf
Oven Temperature: 375° F.
Baking Time: Check after 30 minutes

Ingredients

2 packets active dry yeast
½ cup 90° F. water
2½ cups milk
½ cup butter
1 cup white sugar
½ teaspoon salt
1 extra large egg
6 cups unbleached white flour
1 to 2 cups additional unbleached white flour
optional flavorings: use only one:
1½ to 2 teaspoons cardamom
1 tablespoon grated lemon rind
1 tablespoon grated orange rind
½ teaspoon nutmeg or mace

Extra

butter to grease bowl and baking sheet
glaze
frosting and/or filling

Utensils

glass measuring cup
set of graduated metal measuring cups
set of measuring spoons
bread bowl
small bowl
flour sifter
electric mixer
medium saucepan
clean kitchen towel
kitchen thermometer
wire whisk
baking sheet or 2 bread pans
kitchen timer
2 cooling racks
hot pad

Procedure

Mixing

1. Read the chapter introduction.
2. Measure out 2½ cups of milk in a glass measuring cup and pour it in a saucepan. Set the pan aside for a moment and wash out the measuring cup.
3. Run the tap water to a temperature of 90° F. Check it with your thermometer and fill the clean glass measuring cup with ¼ cup of 90° water. Empty the packets of yeast into the water and stir to begin the dissolving process. Set the measuring cup in a warmish, draft-free place. We usually put ours over the pilot light of a gas stove or in a barely warm oven with the door closed.
□ Water cooler than 85° F. will retard the growth of the yeast; water hotter than 110° F. will kill it.
□ Warm the oven by turning it on 200° or low for 1 or 2 minutes and then shutting it off.
4. Place the saucepan on the stove and set flame or burner at low temperature. Stir occasionally until the milk is scalded. (The milk is scalded when a thin skin forms on the surface of the milk and bubbles begin to form around the edges. Do not boil the milk or heat it over a high flame.) Remove the pan from the heat.
□ The scalding process is important because it prevents bacteria in the milk from killing the yeast.
5. Cut the butter into eight to ten pieces. Add them to the scalded milk and stir until they are dissolved. Now add the sugar, salt, and flavoring. Stir to dissolve the sugar. Pour the mixture into the bread bowl and cool it to 90°.

6. Check the yeast and water mixture. All the grains of yeast should be dissolved and turned into a thick, milky, putty-gray substance with bubbles on top. If the yeast mixture does not look like this, discard it and start over again with fresh packets of yeast.

7. Stir the healthy yeast and the egg into the cooled scalded milk mixture.

8. Sift 4 cups of flour into the bowl, 1 cup at a time, beating with the electric mixer or by hand after every addition.

□ This mixing process is important because it begins to develop the gluten structure that will eventually hold up the bread, making it light and tender instead of dense and tough.

9. Allow the dough to rest for 10 minutes. This will make it less sticky when you knead it.

10. Set the bowl on a sturdy counter top at a comfortable height for working the dough in the bowl. Sift 1 cup of flour over the top of the dough and begin kneading in the bowl. This is the way to knead: Starting with the edge of dough closest to you, push the dough away from you lightly with the heels of your hands. Now pull the outside edge over the top of the dough. Turn the dough inside the bowl a quarter-turn and repeat the motions. Continue pushing, pulling, and turning the dough in a nice steady rhythm, curving your fingers around the edge of the dough while you work to prevent excessive flattening.

11. After you have completely worked in the first cup of flour, continue adding flour ½ cup at a time, kneading each flour addition into the dough completely before adding more. You will probably have to discontinue the sifting at this point and scoop the flour directly from the canister with a measuring cup. Work the dough that is stuck to the sides of the bowl and your hands into the large mass of dough while you knead.

12. As the dough becomes less sticky, you may want to remove it from the bowl to a lightly floured board for a final kneading. Continue kneading and adding small amounts of flour to the dough until it is no longer sticky and has a smooth, elastic feel. Air bubbles will begin to form on the surface. You can hear them break as you knead. The amount of flour needed to finish the dough will vary from one batch of bread to another. Don't worry about adding exact amounts of flour, just keep sprinkling small (½ cup) amounts of flour on the dough and working them in until the dough achieves the desired smooth, elastic consistency.

13. Lightly grease the entire inside of the bowl with a tiny amount of the extra butter. Shape the dough into a smooth ball and place it in the bowl with any rough edges on the bottom. Wet a clean kitchen towel and wring out all of the excess water. The towel should not be drippy. Completely cover the top of the bowl with a towel.

Rising
1. Place the dough in a slightly warmed, shut-off oven for approximately 1 hour. Check the dough after ½ hour to be sure the towel is still damp and the oven is warm. The bowl should still be warm to the touch. If the bowl is cold, remove it from the oven and turn the oven on to warm (200°)

for 2 or 3 minutes. Turn the oven off and replace the bowl.

2. The dough will have risen enough when blisters of gas begin to appear on top of the dough and it has doubled in bulk. Press two of your fingers deeply into the dough. If the impression remains, the dough has risen enough.

3. Punch the dough down by plunging your fist into the center. Fold the edges of the dough over from all four sides and punch it down again. Do this two or three times to break up the large gas pockets that formed while the dough was rising. Turn the dough over so the smooth side is up. Allow the dough to rest for 10 minutes.

Shaping

Spiral loaf

To shape a Spiral Loaf you will need cooking oil, a rolling pin, and a pastry brush.

1. Grease a baking sheet or round pan with butter.

2. Rub a very small amount of cooking oil over your working surface and roll the dough out with a rolling pin to a thickness of ¼ inch. The rolled-out dough should be coaxed into an oblong shape, 22 x 15 inches.

3. Beat an egg with 2 tablespoons of water and lightly brush the top of the dough with the beaten egg. Spread your choice of filling over the dough to within about 1 inch from each edge.

4. Roll the dough like a jelly roll and press the outside edge to seal it. You may bake the dough as is, in an oblong shape on a baking sheet, or you may place the dough in a large round pan, pressing the joining ends of the dough to seal it. In either case the dough should be placed with the sealed edge down.

5. Place the dough in a warmed, shut-off oven for ½ hour or until the dough has doubled in bulk.

6. If you like you may cut evenly spaced slashes in the top of the dough. You may coat the risen bread dough with the egg glaze or a sugar glaze, page 54 and 62.

7. Turn the oven on to 375° and set your timer for 30 minutes. Check the bread when the timer goes off. Bake it until it is medium golden brown. Remove the bread from the oven, allow it to cool for 1 or 2 minutes in the pan and remove it to a cooling rack.

8. You may frost (see frosting, page 64) the cooled bread or serve it as is.

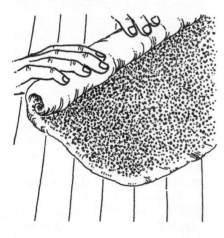

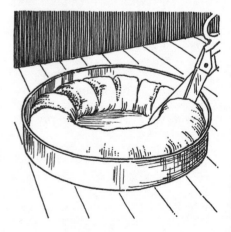

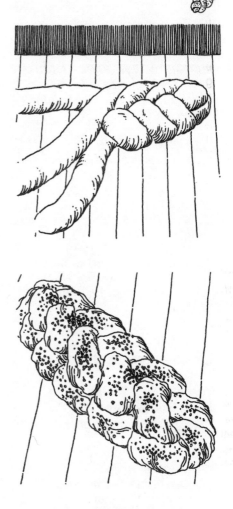

Braided loaf

To shape a Braided Loaf you will need cooking oil.

1. Grease a baking sheet with butter.

2. Rub a very small amount of cooking oil over your working surface. Place the dough on the surface and cut it into three equal pieces. Roll each strip with your hands into a long cigar shape 1½ inches in diameter. Lay the long pieces of dough parallel to each other on the board and press three of the ends together. Braid the three strips of dough and press the ends together. Carefully move the braided dough to the baking sheet. Turn both ends under and arrange the dough attractively on the baking sheet.

3. Place the dough in a warmed, shut-off oven for ½ hour or until the dough has doubled in bulk. If you like you may coat the risen bread dough with a sugar glaze, page 62, or with an egg glaze, page 54.

4. Turn the oven on to 375° and set your timer for 30 minutes. Check the bread when the timer goes off. Bake it until it is medium golden brown. Remove the bread from the oven, allow it to cool for 1 or 2 minutes in the pan, and remove it to a cooling rack.

5. You may frost the cooled bread with a frosting (see page 64).

Rich Sweet Bread

Quantity: *One large free-form loaf*
Oven Temperature: *375° F.*
Baking Time: *Check after 30 minutes*

Ingredients
 2 packets active dry yeast
 ¼ cup 90° F. water
 ¾ cup milk
 ¾ cup butter
 ¾ cup white sugar
 ½ teaspoon salt
 5 extra large egg yolks
 3 cups unbleached white flour
 1½ to 2½ cups additional unbleached white flour

Extra
butter to grease bowl and baking sheet
glaze
frosting and/or filling

Procedure
Follow the directions for Basic Sweet Bread. Beat the egg yolks with a fork to mix them and add them to the cooled liquid ingredients. Shape, fill, and frost as desired.

Christmas Sweet Bread

Quantity: *One free-form loaf*
Oven Temperature: *375° F.*
Baking Time: *Check after 30 minutes*

Ingredients
 1 packet active dry yeast
 ¼ cup 90° F. water
 1 cup milk
 ½ cup butter
 ½ cup white sugar
 ½ teaspoon salt
 1 extra large egg .
 ½ teaspoon ground cardamom
 4 teaspoons grated orange rind
 3 cups unbleached white flour
 1½ to 2 cups additional unbleached white flour

Extra
butter to grease bowl and baking sheet
glaze
frosting and/or filling

Procedure
Follow the directions for Basic Sweet Bread. Beat the egg with a fork to mix it and add it to the cooled liquid ingredients. Add the cardamom and orange rind before adding the flour. Shape, fill, and frost as desired.

Poppy Seed Filling

Quantity: *Filling for one sweet bread recipe*

Ingredients
3 cups poppy seeds
1⅓ cups honey
½ cup unsalted butter
2 cups half-and-half or light cream
6 tablespoons cornstarch

Procedure
Measure all ingredients and place in a saucepan. Bring to a boil and hold mixture at a boil for 1 minute. Stir gently to prevent burning on the bottom of the pan. Cool.

Nut Filling

Quantity: *Filling for one sweet bread recipe*

Ingredients
2½ cups chopped nuts
1 cup honey
½ cup unsalted butter
½ cup half-and-half or light cream
2 tablespoons cornstarch

Procedure
Melt butter in a saucepan. Combine nuts and honey in mixing bowl. Stir in half-and-half, cornstarch, and lastly the melted butter. Cook over medium flame until mixture thickens.

Apricot Filling

Quantity: *Filling for one sweet bread recipe*

Ingredients
½ pound dried apricots
1 cup fresh or reconstituted orange juice
¼ cup honey or brown sugar
1 tablespoon grated orange peel

Procedure
Measure out orange juice, honey, and orange peel and place in a sauce pan. Add apricots and gently simmer—stirring frequently to prevent sticking on the bottom of the pan—until the liquid is absorbed by the apricots. Cool.

Sugar Glaze

Quantity: *Topping for one sweet bread recipe*

Ingredients
cream (either heavy or light)
flavored sugar

Cinnamon sugar
1½ teaspoons cinnamon
½ cup white sugar

Vanilla sugar
Bury 3 or 4 vanilla beans in your white sugar canister. Leave for a few days. Will keep indefinitely.

Orange sugar
2 tablespoons grated orange rind
½ cup white sugar

Lemon sugar
2 tablespoons grated lemon rind
½ cup white sugar

Nutmeg sugar
¼ teaspoon nutmeg
¼ teaspoon mace
½ cup white sugar

Procedure
Use a pastry brush to coat the risen bread with cream and sprinkle with one of the flavored sugars. Bake as directed.

Plain Glaze

Quantity: Glaze for one sweet bread recipe

Ingredients

2 tablespoons soft butter
1 cup powdered sugar
1½ tablespoons milk
½ teaspoon vanilla
1 tablespoon grated lemon or orange rind (optional)

Procedure

Cream the butter with an electric mixer until it is light and fluffy. Gradually add ½ cup powdered sugar. Add the milk and then the balance of the powdered sugar. Beat in the flavorings last. The mixture should be thick enough to allow it to be spread without being runny.

□ Sift the powdered sugar before measuring it to smooth out any little clumps.

Honey Glaze

Quantity: Glaze for one sweet bread recipe

Ingredients

¼ cup soft butter
3 tablespoons honey
1 egg white
¾ cup powdered sugar
1 tablespoon grated lemon or orange rind (optional)

Procedure

Cream the butter with an electric mixer until it is fluffy. Beat the honey into the butter and then gradually add the egg white. Beat in the powdered sugar and grated rind last.

□ Sift the powdered sugar before measuring it to smooth out any little clumps.

Sour Cream Frosting

Quantity: Frosting for one sweet bread recipe

Ingredients
  4 tablespoons soft butter
  ¼ cup sour cream
  1 cup powdered sugar
  1 teaspoon vanilla

Procedure
Cream the butter with an electric mixer until it is fluffy. Beat in the sour cream and then gradually add the powdered sugar. Beat in the vanilla.

□ Sift the powdered sugar before measuring it to smooth out any little clumps.

Tart Lemon Icing

Quantity: One cup icing

Ingredients
  ¼ cup fresh lemon juice
  1¼ cups powdered sugar

Procedure
Squeeze, strain, and measure out the lemon juice and put it in a small bowl. Measure and sift the powdered sugar into the lemon juice. Beat until the mixture is smooth. Spread the icing over the cooled bread immediately. The icing will harden in about 30 minutes.

Chemically Leavened, or "Quick" Breads

Quick bread is a catchall name for an endless variety of oven-baked foods and even a few that are boiled or fried. The thread that ties them all together is the way they are leavened. Most quick breads contain the same basic ingredients found in yeast breads except of course the yeast, which is replaced by a chemical compound: baking powder or baking soda. Either of these leavening agents requires little or no time between the mixing and baking steps—hence the name quick bread.

We have divided quick breads into two basic groups based on the way the ingredients are mixed together. The first group is called batter quick breads. All of these breads use a liquid fat. Muffins are the primary example, although many other common quick breads you may not associate with muffins are based on similar mixing procedures.

The second group is dough quick breads, which are mixed from a solid fat. Biscuits are the most typical example.

Before you begin mixing your quick bread, be sure to set out all the ingredients and utensils you will need on your kitchen counter. If you have all of the proper ingredients and utensils set out before you, most quick breads may be mixed up in minutes.

Muffins

Muffins are the easiest to make of all the batter breads. They require no elaborate mixing procedures or kneading, rolling, and cutting techniques. You simply mix together two groups of ingredients: wet and dry; spoon the batter into a muffin pan; pop the pan into the oven; and in less than ½ hour from start to finish, the muffins are ready to serve.

By varying the amounts of sugar and salt, and with the addition of various flavorings, you may serve them appropriately with any meal.

Mixing the muffins is the critical factor in making beautiful muffins. Incorrect mixing will affect the shape as well as the texture of the muffin.

If the muffins are undermixed, the baking powder will not be completely moistened and the muffins will be flat topped and compact. They will crumble too easily, revealing white spots of flour inside.

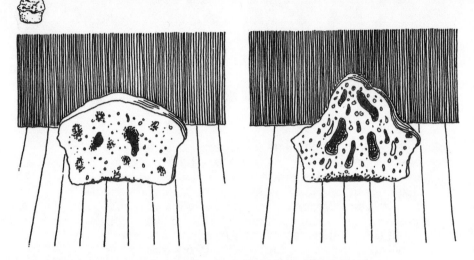

If the muffins are overmixed, the tops will be formed into a large, smooth hump. When you break them open, the interior will be filled with vertical tunnels directed toward the peak. Although this muffin has a fine texture it will be somewhat tough, because the gluten structure of the flour was developed as you overmixed the batter.

A properly mixed muffin is a beautiful golden brown color with a gently rounded, cauliflower textured top and a coarse, tender inside.

Basic Muffins

Quantity: Twelve muffins
Oven Temperature: 425° F.
*Baking Time: Approximately 12
    minutes*

Ingredients

1½ cups sifted all-purpose flour
2¼ teaspoons double-acting bak-
    ing powder
 ¼ teaspoon salt
  3 tablespoons white sugar
  1 extra large egg
 ½ cup milk
 ¼ cup melted butter
    optional variations: add any
    to sifted dry ingredients
  1 teaspoon dill weed
  1 teaspoon caraway seed
  2 tablespoons grated sharp
    Cheddar cheese

Extra

butter for greasing muffin pan

Utensils

glass measuring cup
set of graduated metal measuring
    cups
set of measuring spoons
medium mixing bowl
small mixing bowl
flour sifter
small saucepan
wooden spoon
wire whisk
rubber scraper
muffin pan
waxed paper
kitchen timer
hot pad

Procedure

Preparation

1. Read the section introduction.
2. Preheat the oven to 425° F.
□ Turn the oven on before you
proceed. Muffins take only minutes to put together.

3. Grease the muffin pan generously with the extra butter.
□ Use a good quality heavy-duty
muffin pan to ensure even heat
distribution while the batter is
baking.
4. Set out all the ingredients and
utensils in a convenient working
space.

Mixing

1. Melt the butter in a saucepan
at a low temperature on the stove.
Remove and set aside to cool
slightly.

2. Tear off two pieces of waxed
paper approximately 12 inches
long. With a metal measuring cup
roughly measure out 2 cups of
flour and sift the flour once using
the waxed paper to catch it.
3. Place the sifter on the second
sheet of waxed paper and measure into it the sugar, salt, baking
powder, and flour. Pour any excess flour back into its storage
container.
4. Sift the dry ingredients onto
the waxed paper; carefully pick
up the piece of waxed paper, and
return the dry ingredients to the

sifter. Sift them into the medium mixing bowl.

□ The second sifting is to ensure complete mixing of the dry ingredients.

5. Break the egg into the small bowl and beat it with a wire whisk or fork until the white and yolk are thoroughly combined.

6. Measure the milk in a glass measuring cup and stir it into the beaten egg.

7. Measure the melted butter and stir it into the egg and milk mixture.

□ Melted and solid butter have different volumes. You must measure the butter after it has been melted.

8. Make a small well in the center of the dry ingredients and pour the liquid ingredients into the well.

□ The well makes it easier to moisten all of the dry ingredients with a minimum of stirring.

9. With the mixing spoon, stir only enough to dampen all of the dry ingredients. The batter should be lumpy.

10. Carefully spoon the batter into the wells of the muffin pan, filling each well two-thirds full of batter.

□ Move the batter around as little as possible. Any movement is a continuation of the mixing process.

11. Fill empty wells in the muffin pan with water to maintain even heating throughout the pan.

Baking

1. Immediately place the muffin pan in the center of the top rack of the 425° oven and set your timer for 12 minutes.

2. Check the muffins when the timer goes off. If the muffins are not golden brown, leave them in the oven a few more minutes.

3. Remove the muffin pan from the oven and allow the muffins to cool 3 to 4 minutes. The muffins should lift easily out of the pan. If they seem to stick, carefully lift them out with a table knife. All muffins must be removed from the pan. If they are allowed to cool in the pan, the bottoms will become soggy.

□ For short periods of time you may tip the muffins to one side in the well of the pan. This allows air to circulate all around the muffins. Cover the pan with a clean towel to keep the muffins warm.

□ Muffins may be baked ahead and reheated. To reheat muffins wrap them tightly in aluminum foil and put them in a 350° oven for 15 minutes.

□ Muffin batter may be mixed a few minutes before actual baking time. Try not to let the batter sit unbaked for more than 20 minutes.

Green Olive and Pecan Muffins

Quantity: Twelve muffins
Oven Temperature: 425° F.
Baking Time: Approximately 14 minutes

Ingredients

1½ cups sifted all-purpose flour
2¼ teaspoons double-acting baking powder
¼ teaspoon salt
2 tablespoons white sugar
1 extra large egg
⅔ cup milk
¼ cup melted butter
8 large green olives, coarsely chopped
½ cup pecans, coarsely chopped

Extra

butter for greasing muffin pan

Procedure

Follow the directions for Basic Muffins with the following additions:

1. Chop the olives and add them to the sifted dry ingredients.

2. Measure the pecans and add to the sifted dry ingredients.

Cinnamon Muffins

Quantity: *Twelve muffins*
Oven Temperature: *425° F.*
Baking Time: *Approximately 12 minutes*

Ingredients
1½ cups sifted all-purpose flour
2¼ teaspoons double-acting baking powder
¼ teaspoon salt
⅓ cup white sugar
½ teaspoon nutmeg
1 extra large egg
½ cup milk
¼ cup melted butter

Topping
⅓ cup melted butter
1 teaspoon cinnamon
⅓ cup white sugar

Extra
butter for greasing muffin pan

Procedure
Follow the directions for Basic Muffins with the following additions:

1. While the muffins are in the oven, melt the butter for the topping over a low flame.
2. Measure the cinnamon and sugar into a small bowl and mix them thoroughly.
3. When the muffins have cooled 3 or 4 minutes, remove them from the pan to a rack. Dip the top of each muffin first in the pan of melted butter and then in the cinnamon and sugar mixture. These muffins are best served warm.

Fresh Berry Muffins

Quantity: *Twelve muffins*
Oven Temperature: *425° F.*
Baking Time: *Approximately 18 minutes*

Ingredients
1½ cups sifted all-purpose flour
2¼ teaspoons double-acting baking powder
¼ teaspoon salt
½ cup brown sugar
1 extra large egg
½ cup milk
¼ cup melted butter
1½ cups coarsely cut strawberries or whole blueberries or whole raspberries

Procedure
Follow the directions for Basic Muffins with the following additions:

1. Clean and measure out the berries. Be sure to drain off all water used to clean them.
2. Add the berries to the sifted dry ingredients. Carefully mix the wet and dry ingredients without mashing the berries.
□ The addition of berries may increase the volume of batter. If you do not have 2 muffin pans and cannot bake all the batter at the same time, be sure to bake the extra batter as soon as the first pan of muffins is finished. If you use 2 muffin pans, do not place 1 pan under the other in the oven. Stagger the pans for even heat distribution. Remember to fill empty wells in the muffin pans with water.
3. Dust the tops of the finished muffins with powdered sugar.

Loaf Quick Breads

These include corn breads and fruit or nut breads. All of
them are mixed using the muffin principle of combined liquid
ingredients added to the sifted combined dry ingredients.

With nut breads being the only exception, the breads in
this group are best served hot from the oven. Nut breads are
easier to slice and have a more mellow flavor if they are
stored for 1 day.

Corn Bread

Quantity: One 9 x 5 inch loaf
Oven Temperature: 400° F.
Baking Time: 30 minutes

Ingredients
    1 cup all-purpose flour
    ¾ cup yellow cornmeal
    3 teaspoons double-acting bak-
        ing powder
    ½ teaspoon salt
    2 tablespoons white sugar
    1 extra large egg
    1 cup milk
    3 tablespoons butter

Extra
butter for greasing the bottom of
    the pan

Utensils
glass measuring cup
set of graduated metal measuring
    cups
set of measuring spoons
medium mixing bowl
small mixing bowl
flour sifter
small saucepan
wooden spoon
wire whisk
rubber scraper
bread pan
waxed paper
kitchen timer
cooling rack
hot pad

Procedure

Preparation
1. Read the section introduction.
2. Preheat the oven to 400°.
3. Grease only the bottom of a
regular bread pan or a quick
bread pan generously with butter.
4. Set out all of the ingredients
and utensils in a convenient working space.

Mixing
1. Melt the butter in a saucepan
at a low temperature on the stove.
Remove and set aside.
2. Tear off two pieces of waxed
paper approximately 12 inches
long. With a metal measuring cup
roughly measure out 2 cups of

flour and sift the flour once using the waxed paper to catch it.

3. Place the sifter on the second sheet of waxed paper and measure into it the sugar, baking powder, salt, cornmeal, and the sifted flour. Pour any excess flour back into its storage container.

4. Sift the dry ingredients onto the waxed paper. Carefully pick up the piece of waxed paper and return the dry ingredients to the sifter. Sift them into the medium mixing bowl.

□ The second sifting is to ensure complete mixing of the dry ingredients.

5. Break the egg into a small bowl and beat it with a wire whisk or fork until the white and yolk are thoroughly combined.

6. Measure the milk in a glass measuring cup and stir it into the beaten egg.

7. Measure the melted butter and stir it into the egg and milk mixture.

8. Make a small well in the center of the dry ingredients. Pour the liquid ingredients into the well.

9. With a mixing spoon, stir only enough to moisten all of the dry ingredients.

10. Scrape the batter into the prepared pan and smooth it into all of the corners.

Baking

1. Immediately place the pan in the center position on the top rack of the oven and set your timer for 30 minutes.

2. Check the corn bread when the timer goes off. If it is not golden brown, return it to the oven for a few more minutes.

3. Remove the corn bread from the oven and allow it to cool 1 or 2 minutes before removing it from the pan. Cut the sides free with a knife or spatula. Turn the pan on its side and bang it against the counter. The bread should come free from the pan.

4. Slice with a warm serrated knife. Serve warm.

Nut Bread

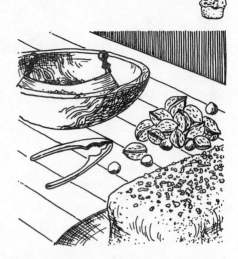

Quantity: One 12 x 3½ inch loaf
Oven Temperature: 350° F.
Baking Time: 1 hour

Ingredients

2½ cups all-purpose flour
1 tablespoon double-acting
    baking powder
½ teaspoon salt
¾ cup white sugar
2 extra large eggs
¾ cup milk
¼ cup butter
1 cup chopped nuts: walnuts,
    filberts, pecans, almonds,
    or cashews

Extra

butter for greasing the bottom of
the pan
2 tablespoons extra nuts to garnish the top of the loaf

Procedure

Follow the directions for Corn
Bread. Note the changes in oven
temperature and baking time.
Carefully add nuts after combining liquid and dry ingredients. Do
not overmix. Chop the extra nuts
a little finer and sprinkle them on
top of the bread before baking.

Indian Pumpkin Bread

Quantity: One 12 x 3½ inch loaf
Oven Temperature: 350° F.
Baking Time: 1 hour

Ingredients

2½ cups all-purpose flour
¼ cup white cornmeal
2 teaspoons double-acting baking powder
1 teaspoon baking soda
½ teaspoon salt
1 teaspoon cinnamon
½ teaspoon ginger
½ teaspoon nutmeg
1 tablespoon grated orange rind
⅓ cup white sugar
1 cup light molasses
2 extra large eggs
¼ cup milk
¼ cup butter
¾ cup canned pumpkin

Extra

butter for greasing the bottom of the pan
chopped nuts for the top of the bread (optional)

Procedure

Preparation

1. Read the section introduction.
2. Preheat the oven to 350°.
3. Generously grease only the bottom of a quick bread pan with butter.
4. Set out all of the ingredients and utensils in a convenient working space.

Mixing

1. Melt the butter in a saucepan at a low temperature on the stove. Remove and set aside.
2. Tear off two pieces of waxed paper approximately 12 inches long. With a metal measuring cup roughly measure out 2½ cups of flour and sift the flour once using the waxed paper to catch it.
3. Place the sifter on the second sheet of waxed paper and measure into it the cornmeal, baking powder, baking soda, salt, sugar, cinnamon, ginger, nutmeg, and flour.
4. Sift the dry ingredients onto the waxed paper. Carefully pick up the piece of waxed paper and return the dry ingredients to the sifter. Sift them into a medium mixing bowl.
5. Break the eggs into a small bowl and beat them with a wire whisk or fork until the whites and yolks are thoroughly combined.
6. Measure the molasses in a glass measuring cup and beat it into the eggs.
□ Dip the measuring cup in very hot or boiling water before measuring the molasses.
7. Measure the pumpkin in metal measuring cups and stir it into the egg and molasses mixture.
8. Measure the melted butter and add it to the liquid ingredients.
9. Grate the orange rind, measure

it, and add to the liquid ingredients.

10. Make a small well in the center of the dry ingredients and pour the liquid ingredients into the well.

11. With a mixing spoon, stir only enough to moisten all of the dry ingredients.

12. Scrape the batter into the prepared pan and smooth it into all of the corners.

13. Sprinkle the top of the bread with chopped nuts.

Baking

1. Immediately place the pan in the center position on the top rack of the oven and set your timer for 30 minutes.

2. Check the bread when the timer goes off. If it is not golden brown, return the bread to the oven for a few more minutes.

3. Remove the bread from the oven and allow it to cool 1 or 2 minutes before removing it from the pan. Cut the sides free with a knife or spatula. Turn the pan on its side and bang it against the counter. The bread should come free from the pan.

4. Slice with a warm serrated knife. Serve warm.

Carrot Bread

Quantity: One 12 x 3½ inch loaf
Oven Temperature: 350° F.
Baking Time: 45 minutes

Ingredients
    2 cups all-purpose flour
 1½ teaspoons double-acting bak-
        ing soda
  ¼ teaspoon salt
    1 cup dark brown sugar
  ½ teaspoon cinnamon
 1⅓ cups water
    1 extra large egg
  ¼ cup butter
    1 tablespoon grated lemon rind
    1 cup shredded raw carrots
    1 cup golden raisins
  ½ cup coarsely chopped
        walnuts

Extra
butter for greasing bottom of the
    pan
poppy seeds for top of loaf

Procedure

Preparation
1. Read the section introduction.
2. Preheat the oven to 350°.
3. Grease only the bottom of a
quick bread pan generously with
butter.
4. Set out all of the ingredients
and utensils in a convenient working space.

Mixing
1. Clean several carrots and grate
them onto a large kitchen plate.
Remove the shredded carrots
from the plate to a measuring cup
using your hand. Squeeze out all
excess juice as you do this. Measure out 1 cup of carrots.
2. Measure the water and raisins
into a heavy saucepan. Add the
carrots and bring the mixture to a

boil over medium heat. Reduce
the heat to low and simmer for 20
minutes, stirring occasionally to
prevent sticking.
3. Remove the pan from the heat
and stir in the butter until it has
melted. Place the pan in a larger
pan partially filled with cold water
to hasten the cooling process.
4. When the mixture has cooled
to lukewarm, grate and measure
the lemon rind and add it to the
mixture.
5. Tear off two pieces of waxed
paper approximately 12 inches
long. With a metal measuring cup
roughly measure out 2 cups of
flour and sift the flour once using
the waxed paper to catch it.
6. Place the sifter on the second
sheet of paper and measure into
it the baking soda, salt, brown
sugar, cinnamon, and flour. Pour
any excess flour back into its
storage container.
7. Sift the dry ingredients onto
the waxed paper. Carefully pick
up the piece of waxed paper and
return the dry ingredients to the
sifter. Sift them into a medium
mixing bowl.

□ The second sifting ensures complete mixing of dry ingredients.

8. Break the egg into a small bowl and beat it with a wire whisk or fork until the white and yolk are thoroughly combined.

9. Make a small well in the center of the dry ingredients. Pour the egg and the carrot mixture into the well.

10. With a mixing spoon, stir only enough to moisten all of the dry ingredients. Carefully stir in the chopped nuts.

11. Scrape the batter into the prepared pan and smooth it into all of the corners. Sprinkle the top of the bread with poppy seeds. Allow the bread to rest for 25 minutes before baking.

Baking

1. Immediately place the pan in the center of the top rack of the oven and set your timer for 45 minutes.

2. Check the carrot bread when the timer goes off. If it is not golden brown, return the bread to the oven for a few more minutes.

3. Remove the carrot bread from the oven and allow it to cool 1 or 2 minutes before removing it from the pan. Cut the sides free with a knife or spatula. Turn the pan on its side and bang it against the counter. The bread should come free from the pan.

4. Cool for 10 minutes. Slice with a warm serrated knife. Serve warm.

Pancakes and Waffles

The batter used to make pancakes and waffles is very similar to muffin batter. The main difference is the thinner consistency of pancake and waffle batter. The methods of cooking the batters are quite different. Muffins are baked in pans in the oven, pancakes are baked in an uncovered frying pan or griddle, and waffles are baked in a special iron.

Pancakes and waffles are most often served as a breakfast dish, but pancakes can also be filled with a variety of cream sauces or cheeses and served as a main course. Topped with fresh fruit and whipped cream, they make a special dessert.

The batter is easily mixed up and keeps well in the refrigerator for up to a week, so it is possible to serve these popular quick breads more frequently than special occasions.

Edward Mulvaney's Pancakes

Quantity: Eight 8-inch pancakes

Ingredients
- 2 cups all-purpose flour
- 1 teaspoon double-acting baking powder
- ½ teaspoon baking soda
- ½ teaspoon salt
- 2 tablespoons white or brown sugar
- 2 extra large eggs
- 2 cups buttermilk (or 1¾ cups sweet milk + 2 tablespoons baking powder; eliminate baking soda)
- 2 tablespoons butter

Extra
butter for wiping frying pan
butter, syrup, jam to serve with pancakes

Utensils
glass measuring cup
set of graduated metal measuring cups
set of measuring spoons
medium mixing bowl
2 small mixing bowls
flour sifter
electric mixer
small saucepan
wooden spoon
rubber scraper
waxed paper
wire whisk
flexible spatula
heavy 10-inch-diameter frying pan
paper towels
hot pad

Procedure

Preparation
1. Read the section introduction.
2. Set out all of the ingredients and utensils in a convenient working space.

Mixing
1. Melt the butter in a saucepan at a low temperature on the stove. Remove and set aside.
2. Tear off two pieces of waxed paper approximately 12 inches long. With a metal measuring cup

roughly measure 2 cups of flour and sift the flour once using the waxed paper to catch it.

3. Place the sifter on the second sheet of waxed paper and measure into it the baking powder, baking soda, salt, and flour. Pour the excess flour back into its storage container.

4. Sift the dry ingredients onto the waxed paper. Carefully pick up the piece of waxed paper and return the dry ingredients to the sifter. Sift them into the medium bowl.

5. Separate the eggs into 2 small bowls. Set the whites aside. Beat the yolks with a wire whisk or fork until they are of an even consistency.

6. Measure the milk in a glass measuring cup and stir it into the beaten egg yolks.

7. Measure the melted butter and stir it into the egg and milk mixture.

8. Make a small well in the center of the dry ingredients. Pour the liquid ingredients into the well.

9. With a mixing spoon, stir only enough to dampen all of the dry ingredients.

10. Beat the egg whites with an electric mixer until they begin to foam. At this stage, large bubbles will gather on the surface and some egg liquid will remain below. Add the sugar at this point and continue beating until the egg whites are stiff enough to hold a peak. Do not overbeat or the egg foam will begin to break apart.

11. Carefully fold the egg whites into the batter until the batter is an even color. Do this immediately because the egg white foam will begin to separate if it is allowed to stand for any length of time.

Cooking

1. Preheat the oven to 250°.

2. Place the heavy frying pan on the stove over a medium heat and melt a small amount, about 1 teaspoon, of the butter in the pan. With a clean paper towel wipe the butter around the pan and remove any excess.

3. Allow the pan to heat up until drops of water sprinkled on the cooking surface dance about.

4. With a ½-cup metal measuring cup, dip the batter from the bowl and carefully pour it onto the hot frying pan. The batter will run out and form a nearly perfect circle.

5. Cook the pancake, watching it carefully, until the top surface is bubbly all over. When the bubbles begin to burst and the edges look dry, turn the pancake. The pancake should be turned only once. To turn a pancake, use a flexible spatula. Carefully slip it under the pancake, lift the pancake, and with good aim return it to the same position in the pan.

6. Check the second side for doneness by lifting a corner of the pancake with the spatula and peeking underneath.

7. When the pancake is done, remove it from the pan to a plate and place it in the oven.

8. Continue wiping the pan with butter, cooking pancakes, and storing them in the oven until the batter is used up. Do this as quickly as possible. Pancakes stacked and stored in the oven too long will dry out on the outside and get soggy on the inside. Or, you may cook only a few pancakes and store the excess batter in the refrigerator for a few days. If you plan to use only half the batter at a time, we recommend dividing the batter in two after you have completed mixing Step 9. Store 1 container of batter and 1 unbeaten egg white in the refrigerator for future use. Beat the second egg white and 1 tablespoon of sugar and fold them into the remaining batter for immediate use.

Swedish Style Pancakes

Quantity: *Eight 8-inch pancakes*

Ingredients
1 cup all-purpose flour
¼ teaspoon salt
1 cup half-and-half
3 extra large eggs
1 cup milk
6 tablespoons melted butter

Extra
butter, syrup, fruit preserves to
  serve with the pancakes

Special utensil
Swedish sectioned pancake pan
  or heavy cast-iron frying pan

Procedure
1. Melt the butter in a saucepan at a low temperature on the stove. Measure it and set it aside.
2. Tear off two pieces of waxed paper approximately 12 inches long. With a metal measuring cup roughly measure 1 cup of flour and sift the flour once using the waxed paper to catch it. Place the sifter on the second sheet of waxed paper and measure into it the flour and salt. Pour the excess flour back into its storage container. Sift the flour and salt once.
3. Beat the eggs until they are of an even consistency. Measure the milk in a glass measuring cup and beat it into the eggs. You may use an electric mixer or eggbeater to do this.
4. Beat the flour and salt in several small additions. Measure and beat the half-and-half. Gradually beat in the melted butter.
5. If you are using a Swedish sectioned pan you will not need to grease it. The batter contains a large amount of butter and will not stick to the pan. If you use a cast-iron pan, melt a small amount of butter in the pan and wipe the butter around the pan with a paper towel. The towel should absorb any excess butter. Heat either pan until drops of water sprinkled on the cooking surface dance about; the pan is ready to cook pancakes. The Swedish pan will hold about 1 tablespoon of batter in each well. (We don't have a Swedish pan so we cook 1 large pancake in a cast-iron pan. To do this, dip the batter from the bowl with a 1-cup measuring cup and carefully pour it onto the cooking surface, tilting the pan to evenly distribute the batter.)
6. The pancakes will bubble and then begin to brown on the edges after 1 or 2 minutes. (You may carefully lift an edge to peek at the brownness of the pancakes underside.) Turn the pancakes and cook 2 minutes on the other side.
7. Serve at once with butter and syrup or fruit preserves.

Basic Waffles

Quantity: Eight 8-inch waffles

Ingredients
- 2 cups all-purpose flour
- 3 teaspoons double-acting baking powder
- ½ teaspoon salt
- 2 tablespoons white or brown sugar
- 3 extra large eggs
- 2 cups milk
- ½ cup butter

Extra
shortening to coat waffle iron
butter, syrup, jam, powdered sugar, fresh fruit to serve with waffles

Special utensils
waffle iron
pastry brush

Procedure

Preparation
1. Read the section introduction.
2. Set out all of the ingredients and utensils in a convenient working space.

Mixing
1. Melt the butter in a saucepan at a low temperature on the stove. Remove and set aside.
2. Tear off two pieces of waxed paper approximately 12 inches long. With a metal measuring cup roughly measure out 2 cups of flour and sift the flour once using the waxed paper to catch it.
3. Place the sifter on the second sheet of waxed paper and measure into it the baking powder, salt, and flour. Pour the excess flour back into its storage container.
4. Sift the dry ingredients onto the waxed paper. Carefully pick up the piece of waxed paper and return the dry ingredients to the sifter. Sift them into the medium bowl.
5. Separate the eggs into 2 small bowls. Set the whites aside. Beat the yolks with a wire whisk or a fork until they are of an even consistency.
6. Measure the milk in a glass measuring cup and stir it into the beaten egg yolks.
7. Measure the melted butter and stir it into the egg yolk and milk mixture.
8. Make a small well in the center of the dry ingredients. Pour the liquid ingredients into the well.
9. With a mixing spoon, stir only enough to dampen all of the dry ingredients.
10. Beat the egg whites with an electric mixer until they begin to foam. At this stage large bubbles will gather on the surface and some egg liquid will remain below. Add the sugar at this point and continue beating until the egg whites are stiff enough to hold a peak. Do not overbeat or the egg foam will begin to break apart.
11. Carefully fold the egg whites into the batter until the batter is an even color. Do this immediately because the egg white foam will begin to separate if it is allowed to stand for any length of time.

Cooking
1. Preheat the oven to 250°.
2. Plug in your waffle iron. Brush it lightly with shortening using your pastry brush to evenly distribute the shortening. Heat the

6. Continue the process of greasing the iron lightly, cooking a waffle and storing it in the oven until all the batter is used up. Serve at once.

iron until drops of cold water splashed on it dance on the cooking surface.

3. Fill a ½-cup metal measuring cup with batter and pour it into the center of the waffle iron. Do not overfill the iron with batter. Too much batter will make a thick, fluffy waffle instead of one with the desired thinness and crispness.

4. Close the waffle lid until steam stops rising from the iron. At this point peek at the waffle. If you want a browner and crisper waffle, leave it in the iron for another 1 or 2 minutes.

5. When the waffle is done, remove it from the iron to a plate and place it in the oven.

7. Unused waffles may be wrapped in a plastic bag and frozen. To thaw, break the waffle into sections and toast them in your toaster. Or, place the waffles in a 350° oven until they are hot.

8. Clean the waffle iron occasionally with a toothbrush and baking soda mixed half and half with water. Wipe the iron clean with a damp cloth. After using this cleaning process, always throw the first waffle baked in the iron away.

Biscuits

Tender, flaky homemade biscuits are a special treat too often replaced with second-rate packaged substitutes. Real biscuits are easy to make and take very little preparation and baking time. There is no real reason to settle for the inferior store-bought variety.

Homemade biscuits may be dressed up in many interesting ways, and with the addition of sugar and a little extra fat make an excellent base for fruit shortcake or cobbler, and breakfast cakes.

Mixing is the critical factor in making a perfect biscuit. The procedure is to cut a solid fat into the combined dry ingredients and then wet this mixture just enough to hold it all together. The coarse crumbs of fat must remain in the finished dough, for these areas of fat are responsible for the flakiness of the finished biscuit. There is no gluten in the fat crumbs and therefore no binding structure, thus the biscuit peels apart in flaky layers. A short period of kneading after mixing will improve the distribution of fat crumbs, but overkneading will break them down and produce tough, solid biscuits.

The perfect biscuit is golden brown with a flat top and straight sides, with horizontal cracks indicating good distribution of fat crumbs. The interior is flaky and tender.

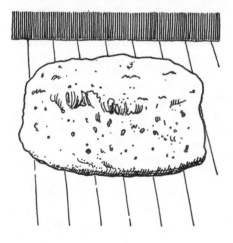

Baking Powder Biscuits

Quantity: Fifteen 3-inch biscuits
Oven Temperature: 425° F.
Baking Time: 15 minutes

Ingredients
    2 cups all-purpose flour
    4 teaspoons double-acting bak-
        ing powder
 ½ teaspoon salt
    1 teaspoon white sugar
 ¼ cup butter or vegetable short-
        ening
 ¾ cup milk

Extra
1 egg white for glaze
poppy or sesame seeds to sprin-
    kle over the top of the biscuits
milk to brush tops of biscuits
flour for pastry cloth

Utensils
glass measuring cup
set of graduated metal measuring
    cups
set of measuring spoons
medium mixing bowl
flour sifter
pastry cloth and rolling pin sleeve
2 knives or pastry cutter
wooden spoon
rolling pin
biscuit cutter or glass of similar
    dimension
pastry brush
baking sheet
waxed paper
kitchen timer
hot pad
metal spatula

Procedure

Preparation
1. Read the section introduction.
2. Plan to have the butter or vegetable shortening at room temper-

ature (70° F.) by the time you are
ready to begin your biscuits.
3. Turn the oven on to 425°.
4. Set out all of the ingredients
and utensils in a convenient working space.

Mixing
1. Tear off two pieces of waxed
paper approximately 12 inches
long. Place the flour sifter on one
of the pieces of waxed paper and
with a metal measuring cup
roughly measure 2 cups of flour
into the sifter. Sift the flour and
move the sifter to the second
sheet of waxed paper. Measure
the flour exactly and put it back
into the sifter. Pour the excess
flour back into its storage

container. Measure the baking
powder, salt, and sugar into the
sifter. Sift the dry ingredients
twice using the waxed paper to
catch the sifted ingredients.
2. Measure the milk in a glass
measuring cup.
3. Measure the butter or vegetable shortening and put it in the
medium mixing bowl.

4. Transfer the sifted dry ingredients to the bowl, and using a pastry cutter or 2 knives, cut the fat into the dry ingredients until the mixture has a uniform coarseness. The crumbs should be the size of barley.

5. Pour the milk into the crumb mixture, and with a fork, mix the ingredients just enough to combine them.

□ Do not overmix the dough. It will quickly become tough and lose its potential for making flaky biscuits.

6. Place the dough on a floured bread board or work surface and knead the dough ten times or less. Stop kneading when the dough holds together in a single ball.

7. Transfer the dough to a floured pastry cloth. See page 98 for preparation of pastry cloth. Cover your rolling pin with a sleeve and begin rolling out the dough. Use quick light strokes, working from the center to the outside in all directions. Do this until the dough has a uniform ½-inch thickness. Flour your biscuit cutter or glass and begin cutting out the biscuits. Flour the cutter as needed.

□ Be sure to press the cutter down evenly or you will have lopsided biscuits.

□ A biscuit cutter has a sharper edge and will cut a better looking biscuit.

8. With a metal spatula transfer the biscuits to an ungreased baking sheet. For crusty biscuits, place the biscuit dough on the sheet leaving at least ¾ inch of space between each biscuit. For soft biscuits place the biscuit dough close together in an ungreased shallow baking pan.

9. Brush the tops of the biscuits with a pastry brush which has been dipped in milk. The milk will dissolve all the little specks of baking powder on the surface of

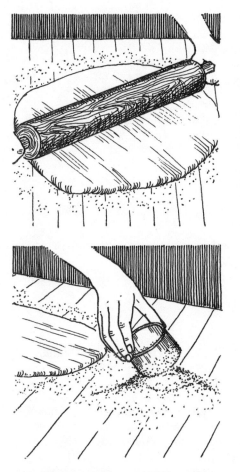

Baking

1. Set your timer for 15 minutes and place the biscuits in the oven.

2. If the biscuits are not golden brown when the timer goes off, return them to the oven for another 1 or 2 minutes.

3. Remove the finished biscuits to a serving basket as soon as they come out of the oven and serve while hot.

the biscuits and give a more uniform golden color to the finished product. Or if you would like to add a special touch to your biscuits, brush the tops with an egg white which has been beaten with a teaspoon of water. Sprinkle poppy or sesame seeds on tops of the biscuits.

☐ If you do this, it will not be necessary to brush the tops with milk.

Buttermilk Biscuits

Quantity: Fifteen 3-inch biscuits
Oven Temperature: 425° F.
Baking Time: 15 minutes

Ingredients
    2 cups all-purpose flour
    1 teaspoon double-acting bak-
        ing powder
    ¼ teaspoon baking soda
    ½ teaspoon salt
    1 teaspoon white sugar
    ¼ cup butter or vegetable short-
        ening
    ¾ cup buttermilk

Extra
milk to brush tops of biscuits
flour for pastry cloth

Procedure
Follow the directions for Baking
Powder Biscuits.

Cheese Biscuits

Quantity: Fifteen 3-inch biscuits
.Oven Temperature: 425° F.
Baking Time: 15 minutes

Ingredients
    2 cups all-purpose flour
    4 teaspoons double-acting bak-
        ing powder
    ½ teaspoon salt
    1 teaspoon white sugar
    1 teaspoon onion powder
    1 teaspoon prepared mustard
        dash cayenne pepper (op-
        tional)
    2 tablespoons grated Parmesan
        cheese or another flavorful
        dry cheese
    ¼ cup butter
    ¾ cup milk

Extra
milk to brush tops of biscuits
flour for pastry cloth

Procedure
Follow the directions for Baking
Powder Biscuits. Add the onion
powder, mustard, and cayenne
pepper to the dry ingredients
before sifting. Add the cheese after sifting.

Oatmeal Biscuits

Quantity: Fifteen 2-inch biscuits
Oven Temperature: 425° F.
Baking Time: 15 minutes

Ingredients
1 cup all-purpose flour
4 teaspoons double-acting baking powder
½ teaspoon salt
1 teaspoon white sugar
1 cup uncooked oatmeal
¾ cup milk
¼ cup butter

Extra
milk to brush tops of biscuits
flour for pastry cloth

Procedure
Follow the directions for Baking Powder Biscuits. Add the oatmeal after the dry ingredients have been sifted.

Biscuit Shortcake

Quantity: Twelve 3-inch biscuits
Oven Temperature: 425° F.
Baking Time: 15 minutes

Ingredients
2 cups all-purpose flour
4 teaspoons double-acting baking powder
½ teaspoon salt
1 tablespoon white sugar
6 tablespoons butter
1 extra large egg
¾ cup milk

Extra
milk to brush tops of biscuits
fresh fruit, sweetened to taste
butter
whipped cream

Procedure
Follow the directions for Baking Powder Biscuits. Beat the egg until it has a uniform color and combine it with the milk. When the biscuits come out of the oven, cut them in half and butter them well. Replace the biscuit top and mound with fresh fruit and whipped cream.

Fruit Cobbler

Quantity: One 9 x 9 inch cobbler
Oven Temperature: 375° F.
Baking Time: 30 minutes

Ingredients

Biscuit Base
    1 cup all-purpose flour
    1 teaspoon double-acting bak-
        ing powder
    ¼ teaspoon salt
    ⅓ white sugar
    3 tablespoons butter
    1 extra large egg
    ¼ cup milk
    3 cups of one of the following
        fruits, sweetened to taste:
        raspberries, blueberries,
        strawberries, or peaches, or
        2 1-pound packages of fro-
        zen berries in syrup

Topping
    ½ cup all-purpose flour
    ½ cup brown sugar
    4 tablespoons butter, or 2 ta-
        blespoons cream cheese
        and 2 tablespoons butter

Special utensil
9 x 9 inch pan

Procedure
1. The biscuit base is mixed following the directions for Baking
Powder Biscuits to Mixing Step 6.
Beat the egg and add it to the
milk. Note the change in oven
temperature.

2. Pat the dough evenly into the
cake pan.
3. Clean the fruit. Cut all large
strawberries in half. Peel and slice
the peaches.
☐ Peaches are much easier to
peel if they are immersed for a
minute in boiling water.
4. Measure the fruit into a medium mixing bowl and sugar it to
your taste. Or, defrost the frozen
berries in a bowl of warm water.
5. Measure the butter or butter
and cream cheese combination
and put it in a medium bowl. Measure the flour and sugar into the
bowl, and using a pastry cutter or
2 knives, cut the mixture together
until it is of a uniform coarseness
with lumps the size of peas.
☐ It is not necessary to sift this
flour before measuring.
6. Spread the fruit evenly over the
biscuit base in the pan.
7. Sprinkle the topping over the
fruit, covering all the fruit with
topping.

Baking
1. Place the pan in the oven and
set your timer for 30 minutes.
2. If the cobbler is not golden
brown when the timer goes off,
return it to the oven for a few
minutes.
3. Remove the cobbler from the
oven, cut it into pieces, and serve
while still warm.

Cynthia DeSchmidt's Dutch Apple Cake

Quantity: One 9 x 9 inch
   breakfast cake
Oven Temperature: 350° F.
Baking Time: 45 minutes

Ingredients
1¼ cups all-purpose flour
   1 teaspoon double-acting bak-
      ing powder
   ¼ teaspoon salt
   ¼ cup white sugar
   ½ cup butter
   1 extra large egg
   1 tablespoon milk
   3 cups sliced tart apples

Topping
1½ tablespoons flour
   ¾ cup white sugar
   ½ teaspoon cinnamon
   2 tablespoons butter

Extra
butter to grease the pan

Special utensil
9 x 9 inch pan

Procedure
1. The biscuit base is mixed following the directions for Baking
Powder Biscuits to Mixing Step 6.
Beat the egg and add it to the
milk. Note the change in oven
temperature.
2. Pat the dough evenly into the
cake pan.
3. Pare, core, and slice the apples. Spread them evenly over the
dough.
4. Measure and mix the topping
ingredients together in a small
bowl. You may use a pastry cutter, 2 knives, or your fingers to do
this. Sprinkle the topping mixture
over the apples.
5. Place the pan in the oven and
set your timer for 45 minutes. If
the cake is not golden brown
when the timer goes off, return it
to the oven for a few minutes.
Serve warm or at room temperature.

Dumplings

Dumplings are closely related to biscuits. The main difference is that dumplings are steamed instead of baked. Dumplings are delicious served with soups and stews, and they are easy to make. However, if dumplings are not mixed and cooked properly, they will be heavy and gummy in the center, or so light they will break apart in the kettle. Follow the mixing instructions and remember not to lift the lid while the dumplings are cooking.

Basic Dumplings

Quantity: *Twelve Dumplings*
Cooking Time: *20 minutes*

Ingredients
2 cups all-purpose flour
2½ teaspoons double-acting baking powder
½ teaspoon salt
2 tablespoons chopped parsley (optional)
1 tablespoon chopped chives (optional)
2 tablespoons butter
1 cup milk

Extra
salt for cooking water

Utensils
glass measuring cup
set of graduated metal measuring cups
set of measuring spoons
medium mixing bowl
flour sifter
4-quart kettle with a tight fitting cover
2 knives or pastry cutter
wooden spoon
slotted spoon
waxed paper

Procedure

Preparation
1. Read the section introduction.
2. Plan to have the butter at room temperature (70° F.) by the time you are ready to begin your dumplings.
3. Fill the kettle with water and add 2 teaspoons of salt. Set the kettle over a medium heat on the stove.
4. Set out all the ingredients and utensils in a convenient working space.

Mixing
1. Tear off two pieces of waxed paper approximately 12 inches long. Place the flour sifter on one of the pieces of waxed paper and with a metal measuring cup roughly measure 2 cups of flour into the sifter. Sift the flour and move the sifter to the second sheet of waxed paper. Measure the flour exactly and put it back into the sifter. Pour the excess flour back into its storage container. Measure the baking powder and salt into the sifter.

Sift the dry ingredients twice using the waxed paper to catch the sifted ingredients.

2. Measure the milk in a glass measuring cup.

3. Measure the butter and put it in a medium mixing bowl.

4. Add the chopped parsley or chives to the flour mixture and transfer the flour to the bowl. Using a pastry cutter or 2 knives, cut the butter into the dry ingredients until the mixture has a uniform coarseness.

5. Pour the milk into the crumb mixture, and with a fork, mix the ingredients just enough to combine them.

6. Flour your hands lightly to keep the dough from sticking to them and shape the dough into walnut-size balls.

Cooking

1. The water in the kettle should be simmering at this time. If it is not, turn the heat up and bring the water to a simmer.

☐ Do not cook the dumplings in water that is rapidly boiling. The action of the water will batter the dumplings around.

2. Drop the dumplings gently into the simmering water. Cover the pot and set your timer for 20 minutes. *Do not* uncover the pot during this time.

3. Heat the stew or soup you wish to serve the dumplings with during the cooking time.

4. When the timer goes off, remove the dumplings from the pot with a slotted spoon and put them in the stew or soup. Serve immediately.

Egg Dumplings

Quantity: Ten Dumplings
Cooking Time: 20 minutes

Ingredients
1½ cups all-purpose flour
1 teaspoon double-acting baking powder
1 teaspoon salt
1 tablespoon butter
1 extra large egg
½ cup milk

Extra
salt for cooking water

Procedure
Follow the directions for Basic Dumplings. Beat the egg until it is a uniform color and add it to the milk. Drop by teaspoonsful into the simmering water.

Doughnuts

Doughnuts may be made from any yeast or quick bread dough that is fried in deep fat. They are best when made with a dough that contains eggs. The eggs will make the doughnuts both rich and light.

It is important not to use excess flour or overmix the dough or the doughnuts will be tough. Also, you must have perfect control over the fat temperature. If the fat is too hot, the doughnuts will not cook through; if it is too cool, the doughnuts will soak up too much fat thereby impairing the flavor and the quality of the finished doughnut. A deep fat cooker with high sides and a regulated temperature control is the only way to properly cook doughnuts.

Basic Doughnuts

Quantity: Two dozen doughnuts
Deep fat temperature: 375° F.

Ingredients
1 cup unbleached white flour
1 cup pastry flour
2 teaspoons double-acting baking powder
½ teaspoon salt
¼ teaspoon cinnamon
¼ teaspoon nutmeg
½ cup brown sugar
2 tablespoons butter
2 extra large eggs
1 extra large egg yolk
⅓ cup milk

Extra
flour for rolling out dough
vegetable shortening or lard for deep frying
powdered sugar or cinnamon sugar to sprinkle on doughnuts

Utensils
glass measuring cup
set of graduated metal measuring cups
set of measuring spoons
medium mixing bowl
3 small mixing bowls
flour sifter
electric mixer
small saucepan
pastry cloth and rolling pin sleeve
rolling pin
wooden spoon
tongs
metal spatula
wire whisk
rubber scraper
2 biscuit cutters of different sizes (2¾- and 1½-inch diameter recommended)
baking sheet
electric deep-fry pan with depth of at least 8 inches and controlled cooking temperature
paper towels
waxed paper
small brown paper bag
cooling rack

Procedure

Preparation
1. Read the section introduction.
2. Set out all the ingredients and utensils in a convenient working space.

Mixing

1. Melt the butter in a saucepan over a low temperature. Remove and set aside.

2. Tear off four pieces of waxed paper approximately 12 inches long. With a metal measuring cup roughly measure out 1 cup of each flour onto separate sheets of waxed paper. Sift them one at a time onto the additional sheets of paper.

3. Place the sifter on a clean sheet of waxed paper and measure into it the baking powder, salt, cinnamon, nutmeg, and 1 cup of each flour. Pour the excess flour back into the appropriate storage containers.

4. Sift these ingredients onto the waxed paper. Carefully pick up the piece of waxed paper and return the ingredients to the sifter. Sift them into the medium bowl.

5. Separate the eggs into small bowls putting 3 egg yolks in one bowl, 2 egg whites in a second bowl, and refrigerating the extra white for future use. Beat the 3 yolks with a wire whisk or fork until they are of an even consistency. Set the 2 whites aside.

6. Measure the milk in a glass measuring cup and stir it into the beaten eggs.

7. Measure the melted butter and stir it into the egg and milk mixture.

8. Make a small well in the center of the dry ingredients and pour the liquid ingredients into the well.

9. With a mixing spoon, stir only enough to dampen all of the dry ingredients.

10. Beat the 2 egg whites with an electric mixer until they begin to foam. At this stage large bubbles will gather on the surface, and some egg liquid will remain below. Begin gradually adding the sugar and continue beating until the egg whites are stiff enough to hold a peak. Do not overbeat or the egg foam will begin to break apart.

11. Carefully fold the egg whites into the batter until the batter is an even color. Do this immediately because the egg white foam will begin to separate if it is allowed to stand for any length of time.

12. Chill the dough for 2 hours in the refrigerator.

□ Chilling the dough will make it easier to roll out and reduce the chances of overworking the dough.

Deep frying

1. Remove the chilled dough from the refrigerator and divide it into four parts. Place one of the parts on a well-floured pastry cloth (page 98) and return the rest of the dough to the refrigerator.

2. Cover the rolling pin with the rolling pin sleeve and dust it with flour.

3. Shape the dough into a perfect little ball with your hands. Do this quickly without overworking the dough.

4. Place the dough in the center of the pastry cloth and begin rolling it out, using quick light strokes. Work from the center to the outside in all directions.

5. Roll the dough to a uniform 1/4-inch thickness. Cut out the doughnuts using a 2¾-inch-diameter round biscuit cutter dipped in flour for the outside cut and a 1½-inch-diameter round biscuit cutter dipped in flour for the inside cut.

□ A glass may substitute for a biscuit cutter, but it will not make as clean a cut.

6. With a metal spatula carefully transfer the cut doughnuts and doughnut holes to a baking sheet and refrigerate. Do not attempt to roll the scraps out a second time. This will only toughen the dough. If you would rather not throw them away, cut them into smaller pieces and fry the odd shapes after you finish the regular doughnut shapes.

7. Continue rolling and cutting the balance of the dough. Store all dough not in immediate use in the refrigerator.

8. Plug in the deep fat fryer. Turn the temperature control to 375°. Place enough vegetable shortening or lard in the cooking well to fill it to a depth of 4 inches.

□ The use of either vegetable shortening or lard is your choice. We ran a test of doughnuts fried in both lard and vegetable shortening and found most of the doughnut testers preferred the vegetable-shortening doughnuts because they were lighter and less greasy. Lard has a very distinctive flavor, which the others preferred.

9. When the deep fat has reached exactly 375°, remove the doughnuts from the refrigerator. Transfer the doughnuts with the metal spatula from the baking sheet to the deep fat one at a time. Do not fill the cooking well with more doughnuts than will fit in the top surface area. The uncooked doughnuts will sink for 1 or 2 minutes when they are first placed in the fat and then rise to the surface.

10. Turn the doughnuts only once. Do this with tongs or cooking fork after the edges of the doughnuts have turned a golden brown. Complete the browning of the second side, lifting the edges of the doughnuts with tongs or fork to check them periodically.

11. Remove the doughnuts to a cooling rack covered with absorbent paper towels. Continue frying the rest of the doughnuts and then fry the holes and scraps. Be sure to watch the fat temperature. It should remain at a constant 375°.

12. While the second batch of doughnuts is frying, shake the first group, one at a time, in a small brown paper bag which contains either powdered sugar or a mixture of granulated white sugar and cinnamon. One teaspoon of cinnamon for each ½ cup of white sugar is a good ratio. Place the finished doughnuts on a plate.

13. When you have finished frying all of your doughnuts, unplug the deep fat fryer and allow the fat to cool. Pour it into an empty jar or coffee can and throw it away, unless you plan to use it again the very same day.

□ After fat has been heated to a high temperature it will rapidly become rancid no matter how it is stored.

Pastry

A tender, flaky pastry crust is the ambition of most good cooks. It seems to be so difficult to achieve that we often hear of new, no-fail recipes for crusts. These recipes usually disappoint us. Don't despair; it is not difficult to make a perfect pastry crust if you understand a few basic principles.

The proper proportions of the main ingredients—flour, water, and fat—are of the utmost importance. Too much fat will make a greasy, crumbly dough that is difficult to roll out and browns unevenly. Too much liquid will make the crust soggy and too sticky to roll out. Too much flour will make it tough.

The proper ingredients are also very important. You must use either all-purpose or pastry flour. You may choose among lard, vegetable shortening, or butter for the fat. In our opinion butter gives a crust the most pleasing flavor and vegetable shortening the most pleasing texture. Lard has a distinctive flavor and a pleasing texture.

A crust must be mixed correctly. The flakiness in pastry is produced by tiny areas of fat in the dough. They are formed when fat is cut into flour. There is no gluten in these fat areas and therefore no binding structure. This causes the crust to flake apart. (The same principle causes flakiness in biscuits.) Overworking the dough will cause the fat areas to dissolve and produce a less flaky crust.

The tenderness of a crust is a function of how much the dough is worked during mixing and rolling out. Any excessive working of the dough develops the gluten structure and toughens the dough. For this reason flour should never be added to the dough after the liquid has been mixed in.

Chilling the dough is the last important factor influencing a good pastry crust. It forces the production of steam when the cold crust is placed in a hot oven. Chilling also reduces shrinkage of the crust and makes it easier to roll out.

Your pastry crust will brown the best in a glass pie pan.

If you follow these tips, you will surely produce a beautiful pastry crust.

Plain Pastry

Quantity: *One 9-inch single crust or one 9-inch double crust*

Pie shell only
Oven Temperature: *425° F.*
Baking Time: *15 minutes*

Ingredients

Single crust
1½ cups all-purpose flour
½ teaspoon salt
6 tablespoons butter or ⅔ cup
   vegetable shortening
2 to 4 tablespoons cold water

Double crust
2 cups all-purpose flour
¾ teaspoons salt
9 tablespoons butter or 1 cup
   vegetable shortening
¼ to ⅓ cup cold water

Filling
4 cups of fruit filling
3½ cups of baked custard filling
4 cups of cooked custard filling
(Meringue instructions given on
   page 185)

Extra

flour to dust pastry cloth
egg white
sugar

Utensils

glass measuring cup
set of graduated metal measuring
   cups
set of measuring spoons
medium mixing bowl
pastry cloth and rolling pin sleeve
rolling pin
knife or spatula
rubber scraper
kitchen scissors
9-inch-diameter glass pie pan
waxed paper
hot pad

Procedure

Preparation

1. Read the chapter introduction.
2. The job of rolling out a pie crust or any other dough will be made easier by the use of a canvas pastry cloth and a rolling pin sleeve. These are packaged and sold together. If you don't already own a set, these are necessary items.

The theory behind the cloth and sleeve is to work flour into them, making a very special surface that, while it does not transfer the flour to the dough, prevents even the softest dough from sticking to it.

3. Prepare and care for a pastry cloth and rolling pin sleeve in the following way:

a. Spread the canvas out on an ample working surface. Roughly measure out ½ cup of all-purpose flour and spill it in the center of the cloth. Rub this flour around the cloth until it is completely absorbed into the cloth. When the flour seems to be gone, scrape the surface of the pastry cloth with the side of a spatula. Work all flour gathered by the spatula back into the cloth.

b. Cover the rolling pin with the pastry sleeve. Rub a handful of flour into the pastry sleeve.

c. Sprinkle a handful of flour on the canvas and rub and roll it in with the covered rolling pin. Scrape the canvas one more time and again work in all loose flour.

d. After using the pastry cloth and sleeve, scrape off all excess flour with a spatula. Roll the cloth around the rolling pin and wrap them in waxed paper. Fasten with a rubber band.

□ When necessary, clean the cloth and sleeve, with a small brush and warm soapy water. Dry them spread out on a flat surface. Do not wring out excess water. Prepare the clean canvas as described in steps a, b, c, and d.

4. Plan to have all of the ingredients at room temperature (70° F.) at the time you are ready to begin. Set out all the ingredients and utensils in a convenient working space.

Mixing

1. Tear off two pieces of waxed paper approximately 12 inches long. Place the flour sifter on one of the pieces of waxed paper and with a metal measuring cup roughly measure out the flour and put it in the sifter. Sift the flour and move the sifter to the second sheet of waxed paper. Measure out the flour and put in the sifter. Return any excess flour to its storage container. Measure the salt and sift it with the flour twice using the waxed paper to catch and transfer the mixture.

2. Measure the water and put it in the glass measuring cup.

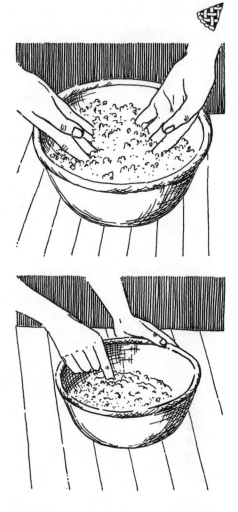

3. Measure the butter or shortening and put it in the medium mixing bowl.

4. Transfer the flour and salt mixture to the bowl. With your fingers work the fat and flour together until it is a uniform coarse mixture of crumbs the size of small peas.

□ Do this efficiently. Overworking the flour and fat will develop the gluten in the flour and cause a tough pie crust. The crumbs of fat produce the flakiness in the finished product.

5. Add the water, and, using your forefingers, stir the dough just enough to allow you to form it into a ball.

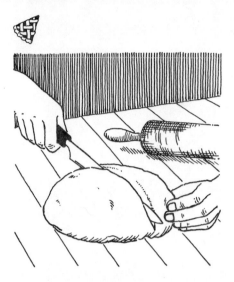

6. If you are making a single crust, gently perfect the shape of the ball, smoothing the edges and closing in any cracks. Wrap the ball of dough in waxed paper and refrigerate it for 2 hours.

7. If you are making a double crust, divide the ball of dough not quite in half. One ball of dough should be slightly larger than the other. The larger ball of dough will be the bottom crust. Smooth the dough as described in Step 6. Wrap and refrigerate it for 2 hours.

Rolling

1. When the dough is thoroughly chilled, remove it from the refrigerator and immediately place it in the center of the prepared pastry cloth. Cover the rolling pin with the sleeve. Roll out the pie crust with quick, light strokes that begin in the center of the dough. Roll toward the edges in all directions lifting the rolling pin slightly as you reach the edge. This action will prevent the edges of the dough from cracking and splitting. Adjust the direction of the rolling pin to keep the dough as close to a perfect circle as possible.

☐ Roll the dough as soon as it is removed from the refrigerator. Chilled dough is easier to work.

□ If the dough sticks, sprinkle it with flour. Do this with care, using as little flour as possible.

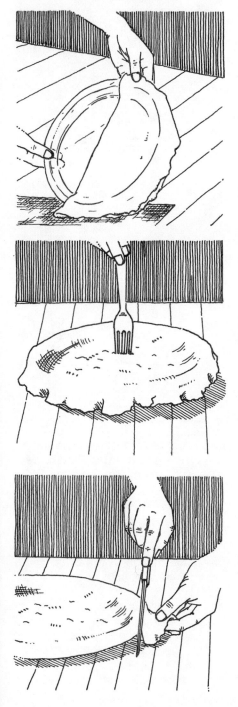

2. Roll the dough to a uniform thickness of ⅛ inch.

3. Carefully fold the dough in half loosening it with a knife or spatula if it sticks to the pastry cloth.

□ Do not pull or stretch the dough, as this action will give the crust a tendency to shrink during baking.

4. Carefully place the dough in the pie pan and unfold it. Fit it into the pan with your fingers.

5. With the tines of a fork, prick all around the sides and bottom of the crust to allow trapped air to escape and prevent the crust from puffing up while baking.

6. With a pair of kitchen scissors or a sharp knife, trim away all excess dough, leaving an overhang of 1 inch for a single-crust pie and ½ inch for a double-crust pie.

7. Turn this overhang under all the way around the pie pan. The finished edge should extend over the edge of the pie pan about ¹⁄₁₆ inch.

□ If the crust cracks or breaks while you are working with it, wet the two edges you wish to rejoin with a small amount of water and gently pat them back together.

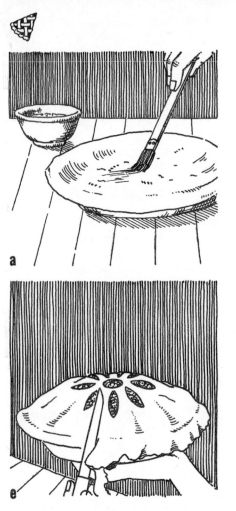

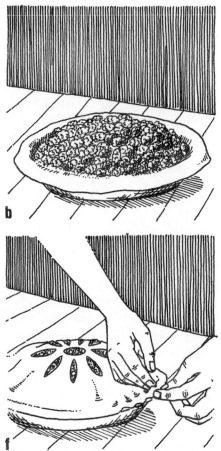

Double-crust pie

8. If you are making a double-crust pie fill the pie pan at this point. Coat the inside of a crust being used with a fruit filling with a thin layer of sugar or brush it with beaten egg white. The sugar or egg white will prevent the bottom crust from becoming soggy.

9. Finish the top of the pie by rolling the second, smaller piece of dough the same way you rolled the first crust. Wet the edges of the bottom crust with a small amount of water. Carefully place the top crust over the filled pie. Trim away the excess crust. The top crust should be cut evenly with the bottom crust. Finish the edges in any of the illustrated ways.

10. With a sharp knife or cookie cutter, cut several air holes in the top crust. Here is a good chance to make the pie special. Cut a seasonal design in the crust or make a pattern with cookie cutters.

11. If you like a shiny pie crust, brush the top and edges of the pie with an egg white beaten with 1 or 2 teaspoons of water. Do this lightly, being careful not to spread the egg white too thickly.

c

d

g

h

12. For a final decorative touch, sprinkle the crust with granulated sugar (coarse sugar works well) or, depending on the filling, with cinnamon sugar or coarsely ground stick cinnamon.
13. Bake as directed by the filling.

Single-crust pie
14. Finish the edges of the crust in one of the illustrated ways. If you like, brush the edges with egg white and dust with sugar as described in Steps 11 and 12. Be careful not to glob the egg white into the low areas of a fluted edge.

15. Fill the pie crust shell and bake as directed by the filling.
16. If your pie has a baked custard filling, you may wish to add the following decoration. With a cookie cutter or a knife, cut out a shape or two from the excess pie crust. Brown these shapes very lightly on a baking sheet while the pie is baking. Position them on top of the pie filling 5 or 10 minutes before it has finished baking.
17. If your pie has a cooked or frozen filling, the pie shell must be baked unfilled. Depending on the shape of your pie pan, this procedure can cause a problem.

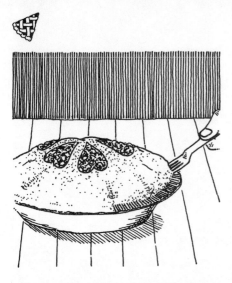

If the pie pan has steep sides, the pie dough will collapse and fall to the bottom of the pan while it is baking. To avoid this problem, line the inside of the un-baked crust with waxed paper and fill it with uncooked rice or beans. Bake the crust for 6 minutes. Remove from the oven. Carefully pour out the rice or beans and pull the waxed-paper liner from the pan. Brush the inside of the crust with an egg white beaten with 1 to 2 table-spoons of water. Return the crust to the oven and complete baking. If your pie pan has a gently slop-ing side, be sure the edge of the crust overlaps all around the edge of the pan before you bake the crust.

□ Remember to set the timer when you place the pie shell in the oven.

□ The egg white glaze will pre-vent the crust from absorbing moisture from the filling (cooked or frozen) and becoming soggy.
□ The rice or beans are not edi-ble after they have been baked in the crust, but they can be stored away and used again for the same purpose.

Cream Cheese Pastry

Quantity: One 9-inch single crust

Ingredients
1¼ cups all-purpose flour
¼ teaspoon salt
1 3-ounce package of cream
   cheese
4 tablespoons butter
2 tablespoons milk

Extra
flour to dust pastry cloth

Procedure
Follow the directions for Plain
Pastry. Sift the sugar with the salt
and flour. Treat the cream cheese
as a fat. Combine the cream
cheese and butter before adding
the flour.

Sweet Pastry

Quantity: One 9-inch single crust

Ingredients
1½ cups all-purpose flour
¼ teaspoon salt
2 tablespoons white sugar
1- 3-ounce package cream
   cheese
8 tablespoons butter
4 tablespoons cold water

Extra
flour to dust pastry cloth

Procedure
Follow the directions for Plain
Pastry. Sift the sugar with the salt
and flour. Treat the cream cheese
as a fat. Combine the cream
cheese and butter before adding
the flour.

Pâte Brisée

Quantity: One 9-inch single crust

Ingredients
1¼ cups all-purpose flour
½ teaspoon salt
6 tablespoons butter
2 tablespoons vegetable shortening
3 to 5 tablespoons cold water

Extra
flour to dust pastry cloth

Procedure
Follow the directions for Plain
Pastry. This dough may be refrigerated for 2 days or frozen for
longer periods of time. Defrost
frozen Pâte Brisée dough in the
refrigerator for 24 hours.

Cakes

A cake is the center of attention at tables set to celebrate many occasions. Birthdays, weddings, anniversaries, and seasonal holidays are all associated with cakes. They can also make any everyday meal very special or add a memorable finishing touch to a dinner party. Every knowledgeable, well-rounded cook should be able to bake a good cake. With a little experience, it is just as easy to make a cake from "scratch" as it is to use one of the packaged mixes. Cake mixes cost more than the raw ingredients. They are risky and can produce a cake of less desirable flavor and texture, for the ingredients may be damaged by standing on the grocer's shelf for long periods of time.

It is not difficult to bake a perfect cake if you use high quality ingredients, proper mixing procedures, high quality pans, and a good oven. The pans should be made from very heavy metal with a shiny surface inside the pan and a dull underside. Old, thin, beaten up, and blackened pans will not conduct heat as well. Your oven must be capable of distributing heat evenly and constantly. For cakes, we feel gas heated ovens are superior to electric ovens.

An additional factor in making a successful cake every time is using the correct size pan. Altering the pan size will seriously affect both the baking time of the cake and the volume. If you don't have the pan size called for in a recipe, and can't find an alternate pan on the substitutions page, either buy the proper sized pan or bake a different cake.

Cakes are classified into three groups according to the way they are leavened. These are:

Air foam cakes—cakes leavened completely by air.
Butter base cakes—cakes leavened by the chemical leaveners, baking soda and baking powder.
Air foam/butter base cakes—cakes leavened by both air and the chemical leaveners.

The introduction at the beginning of each group of cakes will tell you more about them.

Air Foam Cakes

Air foam cakes are light and delicate. They are leavened entirely by air that is beaten into eggs. An angel food cake is mixed from flour, sugar, and an egg white foam. A sponge cake is mixed from flour, sugar, and both egg white and egg yolk foams. Angel cakes contain no fat. Sponge cakes usually contain only the fat found in egg yolks.

To make either of these cakes successfully, it is important to understand egg foams:

1. The eggs should be at room temperature when they are beaten.

2. To increase the stability of the egg foam, the egg whites are beaten with sugar and an acid, usually cream of tartar; the yolks with sugar.

3. There can be no fat in egg whites or they will not foam.

4. Egg white foams should be beaten only to the soft peak stage. This is important because at this stage they are still flexible enough to combine successfully with the other ingredients. More important, the little bubbles of air incorporated into the egg white have not stretched the white to the maximum yet. This means the egg white structure will still be able to expand when it is baked.

Basic Angel Food Cake

Quantity: One 8-inch cake
Oven Temperature: 350° F.
Baking Time: 45 minutes

Ingredients
  1 cup cake flour
  ¼ teaspoon salt
  1½ cups powdered sugar or su-
       perfine white sugar
  12 egg whites or enough egg
       whites to measure 1½ cups
  1 teaspoon cream of tartar
  1 teaspoon vanilla

Extra
powdered sugar to dust top of
cake

Utensils
glass measuring cup
set of graduated metal measuring
  cups
set of measuring spoons
2 medium mixing bowls (not
  plastic)
flour sifter
electric mixer
rubber scraper
wire whisk
spatula
8-inch-diameter angel food cake
  pan with supports, or a bottle
  or funnel, for inverting the cake
  while it cools
waxed paper
kitchen timer

Procedure

Preparation
1. Read the section introduction.
2. One hour before the time you
have set aside to mix an angel
cake, remove the eggs from the
refrigerator. Separate them while
they are cold. For this, you will
need 2 small bowls and a 2-cup
glass measuring cup, all of them
clean and grease free. Crack the
first egg and split it in half over
one of the bowls. Some of the
white will drop in the bowl immediately. Hold the yolk in half of
the shell, and by transferring it
back and forth from shell to shell,
drain out the rest of the white.
Drop the yolk into the second
empty bowl and with your finger
scrape out any white still remaining in the shells. Pour each yolk-
free white into the glass measuring cup. Repeat the process for
each egg until the volume of
white in the measuring cup is
equal to 1½ cups. Set the egg
whites aside until they reach room
temperature. Refrigerate the yolks
for future use.
□ Never put egg whites in a
plastic bowl.
□ The egg white should be completely free of any traces of the
fat-containing egg yolk. Remove
any specks of egg yolk from the
white with a piece of broken eggshell.
□ If by some misfortune the egg
yolk breaks and spills completely
into the white, transfer this egg to
a storage container and refriger-

ate it for future use in a whole egg mixture. Wash out the bowl and begin again.

3. Set out all the ingredients and utensils in a convenient working space.

Mixing and baking

1. Turn the oven on to 350°.

2. Tear off two pieces of waxed paper approximately 12 inches long. With a metal measuring cup, roughly measure out the flour and sift it onto one of the pieces of waxed paper. Move the sifter to the second sheet of waxed paper and measure the flour, salt, and ½ cup of powdered sugar into the sifter. Pour the excess flour back into its storage container. Run the dry ingredients through the sifter twice using the waxed paper to catch and transfer them. Set the flour mixture aside.

3. Pour the egg whites into a deep straight-sided bowl that is not made from plastic. The bowl should have no traces of grease left in it from previous use. Measure out the remaining cup of powdered sugar and set it next to the electric mixer with the cream of tartar, vanilla, and measuring spoons.

4. Begin beating the egg whites with your electric mixer set on high speed. In a short time, large air bubbles will form on the top of the egg whites while some liquid remains on the bottom of the bowl. The egg whites should still be fluid and transparent. Stop the mixer for a minute and measure and add the cream of tartar, vanilla, and 2 or 3 tablespoons of the previously measured sugar to the egg whites. Turn the mixer on to high and continue beating while adding the balance of the powdered sugar, tablespoon by tablespoon.

☐ Be sure the beaters for your electric mixer are completely grease free.

☐ Don't dump the sugar in all at once; you must gradually add it to the egg whites.

5. In 1 or 2 minutes stop the mixer and pull out the beaters. The egg whites should have reached the soft peak stage by now. The bubbles should be getting smaller and the foam white. As you remove the beaters, the egg white that follows the beaters out of the mixture will bend over into soft curls.

6. Remove the egg whites from

the mixer as soon as the soft peak stage is reached and do the following immediately. Sift about ⅓ of the flour mixture on top of the egg whites, and, using a spatula or wire whisk, gently fold the flour into the egg whites. Folding is accomplished by cutting through the egg white batter, lifting up a portion of it and turning it over. Repeat this motion four or five times turning the bowl slightly each time. Sift the remaining flour over the batter and continue folding until there are no traces of the flour mixture left.

□ The whites will rapidly lose their volume if they are allowed to stand after they are beaten.

7. Hold the bowl over the ungreased angel food pan and gently pour the batter into the pan. Rotate the pan as you do this to evenly distribute the batter. With the spatula, cut through the batter to break up any large air bubbles and spread the batter to an even level in the pan.

8. Immediately place the cake pan in the center of the bottom rack in the oven. Set your timer for 45 minutes. Do not open the oven door until the timer goes off.

9. When the timer goes off, check the cake for doneness by pressing the top surface lightly with your finger. The cake should spring back when the finger is removed. If it does not, return the cake to the oven for a few more minutes.

10. When the cake is done, remove it from the oven and immediately invert the pan. Most angel food cake pans are manufactured with three supports around the top rim. These supports will hold the cake above the cooling surface, allowing the air to circulate all around the cake. If your pan

does not have supports, place it over the neck of a bottle or a funnel as illustrated.

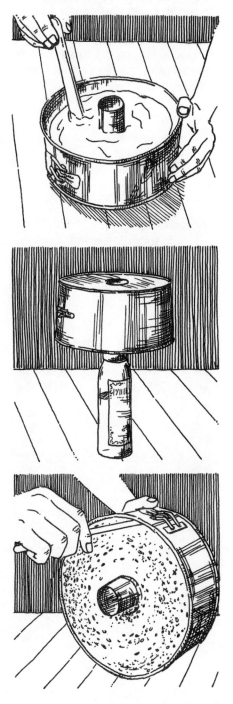

11. After the cake has cooled (the pan should no longer be warm to the touch), turn the pan right side up. Loosen the cake from the sides and center tube of the pan with a spatula. Push the bottom up and out of the pan. Carefully loosen the cake from the bottom with a knife and lift it to a serving plate. Or, invert the pan over a serving plate and ease the cake out with your spatula.

12. Sift powdered sugar over the top of the cake or frost. We recommend Whipped Cream Frosting.

13. Cut the angel cake with a knife that has a serrated edge. Use a gentle back and forth motion to cut the cake. Do not press down heavily on the knife; you will squash the cake.

Whipped Cream Frosting

Quantity: Three cups of frosting

Ingredients
1 cup superfine white sugar
1 cup heavy whipping cream (½ pint)
1 teaspoon vanilla
fresh fruit

Procedure
Measure out the chilled cream. Pour it in the mixing bowl. Beat the cream with the electric mixer set on high until it is so thick that a path made by drawing the rubber scraper through the cream will remain. Gradually add the sugar while continuing to beat the cream with the mixer set on low. Add the vanilla and beat until blended. Spread on the cake with a spatula. Decorate with fresh fruit.

This cake should be served immediately after frosting, and any leftover cake stored in the refrigerator.

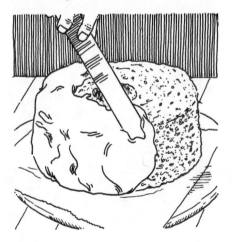

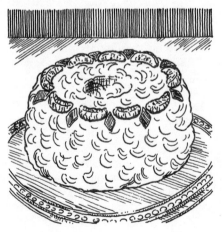

Caramel Angel Food Cake

Quantity: One 8-inch cake
Oven Temperature: 350° F.
Baking Time: 40 minutes

Extra
powdered sugar to dust the top
  of the cake

Ingredients
  1 cup cake flour
  ¼ teaspoon salt
  1¼ cups light brown sugar
  ¼ cup superfine white sugar
  12 extra large egg whites (or
      enough egg whites to mea-
      sure 1½ cups)
  1 teaspoon cream of tartar
  1 teaspoon vanilla

Procedure
Follow the directions for Basic
Angel Food Cake. Sift twice ½
cup of the brown sugar with the
flour. Sift the remaining ¾ cup of
brown sugar with the ¼ cup superfine white sugar twice.

Cocoa Angel Food Cake

Quantity: One 8-inch cake
Oven Temperature: 350° F.
Baking Time: 45 minutes

Extra
half and half mixture of powdered
  sugar and unsweetened cocoa
  to dust the top of the cake

Ingredients
  ¾ cup cake flour
  ¼ cup unsweetened cocoa
  ¼ teaspoon salt
  1½ cups powdered sugar or su-
      perfine white sugar
  12 extra large egg whites (or
      enough egg whites to mea-
      sure 1½ cups)
  1 teaspoon cream of tartar
  1 teaspoon vanilla

Procedure
Follow the directions for Basic
Angel Food Cake. Measure and
sift the cocoa with the flour. Dust
the cooled cake with the half and
half mixture of powdered sugar
and cocoa.

Basic Sponge Cake

Quantity: One 10-inch cake
Oven Temperature: 350° F.
Baking Time: 50 minutes

Ingredients
1½ cups cake flour
 1 teaspoon baking powder
 ½ teaspoon salt
 2 cups white sugar
10 extra large eggs
 1 teaspoon cream of tartar
 1 teaspoon grated lemon rind
 1 tablespoon lemon juice

Extra
powdered sugar to dust top of
 cake
fresh fruit and whipped cream

Special utensils
10-inch-diameter angel food cake
 pan with supports, or a bottle
 or funnel, for inverting the cake
 while it cools

Procedure
1. Read the section introduction.
Follow the directions for Basic
Angel Food Cake through Mixing
and baking Step 2.
2. Measure out ½ cup of sugar
and place it next to your electric
mixer. Begin beating the egg
yolks with the mixer set on high
speed. Gradually add the ½ cup
of sugar and continue beating the
yolks until they become a pale
yellow. This will take several minutes. Mix in the lemon rind and
lemon juice. At this point turn off
the mixer and lift the beaters out
of the bowl. The egg yolk mixture
should be very thick and creamy,
flowing in a thick stream back
into the bowl and mounding on
top of the mixture in the bowl.

When the yolks reach this consistency, set them aside.
3. Remove the beaters from the
mixer and carefully wash them
with hot, soapy water. Dry and return them to the mixer. Pour the
egg whites into a large deep,
straight-sided, grease-free bowl.
Measure out the remaining cup of
sugar and set it next to the electric mixer with the cream of tartar
and measuring spoons.
4. Begin beating the egg whites
with your electric mixer set on
high speed. In a short time large
air bubbles will form on the top of
the egg whites while some liquid
remains on the bottom of the
bowl. The egg whites should still
be fluid and transparent. Stop the
mixer for a minute and measure
and add the cream of tartar and 2
or 3 tablespoons of the previously
measured 1 cup of sugar to the
egg whites. Turn the mixer on to
high and continue beating while
adding the balance of the sugar,
tablespoon by tablespoon.
□ Don't dump the sugar in all at
once; you must add it gradually to
the egg whites.
5. In 1 or 2 minutes, stop the
mixer and pull out the beaters.
The egg whites should have
reached the soft peak stage by
now. The bubbles should be getting smaller and the foam white.
As you remove the beaters the
egg white that follows the beaters
out of the mixture will bend over
in soft curls.
6. Remove the egg whites from
the mixer as soon as the soft
peak stage is reached and do the
following immediately: gently fold
the beaten egg yolks into the egg
whites using a spatula or wire
whisk. Folding is accomplished by

cutting through the egg whites, lifting up a portion of them and turning this over. Repeat this motion four or five times turning the bowl slightly each time. Do this until the egg mixture is an even color.

□ The whites will rapidly lose their volume if they are allowed to stand.

7. Now sift about ⅓ of the flour mixture over the combined beaten eggs. Fold the flour mixture into the egg in the same way. Sift the remaining flour mixture over the eggs and continue folding until there are no traces of the flour mixture left.

8. Hold the bowl over the ungreased angel food pan and gently pour the batter into the pan. Rotate the pan as you do this to evenly distribute the batter. Cut through the batter with the spatula to break up any large air bubbles and spread the batter to an even level in the pan.

9. Immediately place the cake pan in the center of the bottom rack of the oven. Set your timer for 45 minutes. Do not open the oven door until the timer goes off.

10. When the timer goes off, check the cake for doneness by pressing the top surface lightly with your finger. The cake should spring back when the finger is removed. If it does not, return the cake to the oven for a few more minutes.

11. When the cake is done, remove it from the oven and immediately invert the pan. Most angel food cake pans are manufactured with three supports around the top rim. These supports will hold the cake above the cooling surface, allowing the air to circulate all around the cake. If your pan does not have supports, place it over the neck of a bottle or funnel.

12. After the cake has cooled (the pan should no longer be warm to the touch), turn the pan right side up. Loosen the cake from the sides and center tube of the pan with a spatula. Push the bottom up and out of the pan. Loosen the cake from the bottom with a knife, and lift it to a serving plate. Or, invert the cake over a serving plate and ease the cake out with your spatula.

13. Sift powdered sugar over the top of the cake or serve it with fresh fruit and Whipped Cream Frosting, page 112.

Sunshine Sponge Cake

Quantity: One 10-inch cake
Oven Temperature: 350° F.
Baking Time: 50 minutes

Ingredients
1¼ cups cake flour
¼ teaspoon salt
1½ cups powdered sugar
12 extra large egg whites
7 extra large egg yolks
1 teaspoon cream of tartar
1 tablespoon concentrated
   orange juice
grated rind of 1 orange

Extra
1 recipe Boiled Icing, page 116

Special utensils
10-inch-diameter angel food cake
pan with supports, or a bottle
or funnel, for inverting the cake
while it cools

Procedure
Follow the directions for Sponge
Cake. Add the orange juice to the
egg yolks with ½ cup of the
sugar. Add the cream of tartar to
the egg whites with ½ cup of
sugar. Sift the remaining ½ cup
sugar with the flour and salt. Fold
the grated orange rind in with the
flour mixture. Frost the cooled
cake with Boiled Icing.

Boiled Icing

Quantity: One cup icing

Ingredients
¾ cup superfine white sugar
1 extra large egg white
3 tablespoons water
⅛ teaspoon cream of tartar
1 teaspoon vanilla

Special utensils
double boiler
rotary eggbeater

Procedure
1. Fill the bottom pan of the
double boiler with water and
place it over a medium heat.
Bring the water to a slow boil.
2. In the top half of the double
boiler, place the egg white and
water. Measure the sugar and
place it near the stove with the
cream of tartar and measuring
spoons.
3. Place the top half of the
double boiler over the bottom half
and begin beating the egg white
with the rotary beater. When large
bubbles appear on the surface,
add the cream of tartar and the
sugar. Continue beating over the
heat for 7 minutes.
□ Set your timer to clock the time.
4. Remove the pan from the heat
and stir with a spoon until the icing cools. Stir in the vanilla.
5. As soon as the frosting cools
enough to hold its shape, spread
it on the cake with a spatula.

Hot Milk Sponge Cake

Quantity: One 8 x 8 inch cake
Oven Temperature: 375° F.
Baking Time: 30 minutes

Ingredients

Cake
- 1 cup all-purpose flour
- 1 teaspoon double-acting baking powder
- ½ teaspoon salt
- 1 cup white sugar
- 1 tablespoon butter
- 2 extra large eggs
- ½ cup milk
- ½ teaspoon vanilla

Broiled topping
- ½ cup brown sugar
- 3 tablespoons melted butter
- 2 tablespoons light or heavy cream
- ½ cup shredded fresh coconut

Extra

butter to grease the bottom of the pan

Procedure

Preparation

1. Read the section introduction.
2. Set the eggs and butter out 1 hour before you are ready to begin mixing the cake.
3. Set out all the ingredients and utensils in a convenient working space. Turn the oven on to 375°. Grease only the bottom of the cake pan with butter.

Mixing and baking

1. Tear off two pieces of waxed paper approximately 12 inches long. With a metal measuring cup roughly measure out the flour and sift it onto one of the pieces of waxed paper. Move the sifter to the second sheet of waxed paper and measure the flour, salt, and baking powder. Pour the excess flour back into its storage container. Run the dry ingredients through the sifter twice using the waxed paper to catch and transfer them. Set the flour mixture aside.
2. Measure out the milk in a glass measuring cup. Pour it into the small saucepan and scald the milk (see page 29) over a low flame on the stove. Add 1 tablespoon butter, and ½ teaspoon salt, and stir the milk until the butter is melted. Set the pan aside.
3. Break the eggs into a medium-size mixing bowl. Beat them with the electric mixer until they are a light lemon color. Gradually add the sugar, tablespoon by tablespoon, and continue beating the eggs until they are very thick. Beat in the vanilla.
4. Remove the bowl from the electric mixer and sift in about ⅓ of the flour mixture. Gently fold the flour into the eggs. Folding is accomplished by cutting through the egg foam, lifting up a portion of it, and turning it over. Repeat this motion four or five times, turning the bowl slightly each time. Do this until the mixture is an even color.
5. Sift the remaining flour into the bowl and fold it into the egg foam in the same way. Continue folding until there are no separate traces of flour in the mixture.
6. Gently pour the batter into the pan. Spread it evenly around the pan with the rubber scraper. Place the pan in the center of the top rack of the oven. Set the time for 30 minutes.

117

7. Prepare the broiled topping by melting the butter over a low flame on the stove. Stir in the cream, brown sugar, and coconut.

8. When the timer goes off, test the cake for doneness by pressing the top lightly with your finger. The cake should spring back when the finger is removed.

If it does not, return the cake to the oven for a few minutes.

9. When the cake is done, remove it from the oven and spread the topping evenly over the surface. Place the cake under the broiler about 6 inches from the heat and watch it carefully until the frosting bubbles. Cool the cake on a cooling rack.

Butter Base Cakes

Butter base cakes are leavened by the chemical leaveners, baking powder or baking soda, plus an acid. They have a pleasing texture, the result of creaming air into the butter and sugar. Butter base cakes are usually made with all-purpose flour and granulated white sugar. Butter gives them a texture and flavor superior to those produced with other fats.

If your measuring and mixing procedures are exact and you use only fresh ingredients and the correct pan and oven temperature, good results are guaranteed.

The following checklist will be helpful in overcoming any defects:

□ Coarse texture: This is caused by insufficient creaming of the butter and sugar.

□ Heavy texture: This is caused by extreme overbeating of the batter, which develops the gluten in the flour.

□ Dry cake: The cake is either overbaked or contains too little fat in proportion to the other ingredients.

□ Thick crust: The cake was either overbaked or the oven was too hot.

□ Sticky crust: The cake was baked for an insufficient length of time.

□ Humps or cracks in the top: The oven was too hot.

□ Fallen cake: There are many possible causes of a fallen cake. The oven was too slow or the baking time too short. There was too much fat in the batter in proportion to the other ingredients. There was too much batter in the pan, or the pan was not of a good quality. The oven heat was not constant. This may be caused by opening the oven door before the structure of the cake has set. The cake pan was moved before the cake finished baking.

□ Poor volume: The oven was too hot. The pan size was the wrong size. The sides of the pan were greased.

Salted Peanut Cake

Quantity: One 9 x 13 inch cake
Oven Temperature: 350° F.
Baking Time: 35 minutes

Ingredients

1½ cups all-purpose flour
 1 teaspoon double-acting bak-
    ing powder
 ½ teaspoon baking soda
 ¼ teaspoon salt
 1 cup white sugar
 ½ cup butter
 2 extra large eggs
 1 cup buttermilk or sour milk
 1 teaspoon vanilla
 1 cup coarsely ground salted
    peanuts (peanuts with the
    skins left on add interesting
    color and texture to the
    cake)

Extra

butter to grease the bottom of the
   pan
powdered sugar to dust the top
   of the cake

Utensils

glass measuring cup
set of graduated metal measuring
   cups
set of measuring spoons
medium mixing bowl
flour sifter
electric mixer
nut grinder
wooden spoon
rubber scraper
9 x 13 inch cake pan
waxed paper
kitchen timer
cooling rack
toothpick
hot pad

Procedure

Preparation

1. Read the section introduction.
2. Plan to have all the ingredients
at room temperature at the time
you are ready to begin working,
and set out all of the ingredients
and utensils in a convenient working space.
3. Measure and grind the peanuts
with a nut grinder.
4. Grease only the bottom of the
cake pan with butter.

Mixing and baking

1. Preheat the oven to 350°.
2. Tear off two pieces of waxed
paper approximately 12 inches
long. With a metal measuring cup
roughly measure out the flour and
sift it onto one of the pieces of
waxed paper. Move the sifter to
the second sheet of waxed paper
and measure the flour, baking
powder, and salt into the sifter.
Pour the excess flour back into
the storage container. Run the
dry ingredients through the sifter

twice using the waxed paper to catch and transfer them. Set the flour mixture aside.

3. Measure the butter and put it in a medium mixing bowl. Beat it with the electric mixer on high speed until it is light and fluffy.

4. Gradually beat in the sugar and continue beating for 1 or 2 minutes.

5. Add the eggs to the butter and sugar mixture. Beat just enough to completely mix the ingredients together.

□ Overbeating at this stage will cause curdling.

6. Measure out the buttermilk in a glass measuring cup. Measure and add baking soda to the sour milk. Set it next to the mixer.

7. Add approximately ⅓ of the sifted dry ingredients and beat until the mixture is thoroughly combined. Add ½ of the milk and the vanilla and beat until smooth. Beat in another ⅓ of the flour and then the rest of the milk. Add the last ⅓ of flour and beat for 1 or 2 minutes.

8. With a wooden spoon stir in the peanuts.

9. Pour the batter immediately into the prepared pan and place the cake in the center of the top rack in the oven. Set the timer.

10. When the timer goes off, test the cake for doneness by inserting a toothpick in the center of the cake. If the toothpick comes out clean, the cake is done. If tiny bits of cake adhere to the toothpick, return the cake to the oven for a few minutes.

11. When the cake is done, place it on the cooling rack until it reaches room temperature. While the cake is still warm, sift powdered sugar over the top.

Sour Cherry Cake

Quantity: One 9 x 9 inch cake
Oven Temperature: 350° F.
Baking Time: 35 minutes

Ingredients
1¾ cups all-purpose flour
 1 teaspoon double-acting baking powder
 ½ teaspoon baking soda
 ⅛ teaspoon salt
 1 cup brown sugar
 ½ cup butter
 2 extra large eggs
 1 cup buttermilk or sour milk
1½ teaspoons cinnamon
 1 teaspoon nutmeg
 1 teaspoon vanilla
 1 can drained sour cherries

Extra
butter for greasing the bottom of the pan
powdered sugar to dust the top of the cake

Procedure
Follow the directions for Salted Peanut Cake. Add the spices to the sifted dry ingredients. Fold in the cherries after the last addition of flour.

Toasted Sesame Tea Cake

Quantity: One 9 x 5 inch cake
Oven Temperature: 325° F.
Baking Time: 70 minutes

Ingredients
2½ cups all-purpose flour
2½ teaspoons double-acting bak-
　　ing powder
　1 teaspoon salt
　1 cup white sugar
　½ cup butter
　2 extra large eggs
1¼ cups milk
　½ cup toasted sesame seeds
　1 teaspoon grated lemon rind

Extra
butter for greasing the bottom of
　the pan
sesame seeds to sprinkle on the
　top of the cake

Special utensil
one 9 x 5 inch bread pan

Procedure
Follow the directions for Salted
Peanut Cake. Stir in the sesame
seeds and lemon rind after the
last addition of flour. Sprinkle sesame seeds on top of the cake
before baking it.

Orange Honey Tea Cake

Quantity: One 9 x 5 inch cake
Oven Temperature: 325° F.
Baking Time: 70 minutes

Ingredients
2½ cups all-purpose flour
2½ teaspoons double-acting bak-
　　ing powder
　½ teaspoon baking soda
　½ teaspoon salt
　1 cup honey
　½ cup butter
　2 extra large eggs
　¾ cup orange juice
　　grated rind of 1 orange
　1 cup chopped almonds

Extra
butter for greasing the bottom of
　the pan
powdered sugar to dust the top of
　the cake

Special Utensil
one 9 x 5 inch bread pan

Procedure
Follow the directions for Salted
Peanut Cake. Beat in the honey in
place of the sugar. The orange
juice replaces the milk in Step 7.
Stir in the almonds and grated
orange rind after the last addition
of flour.

122

Upside Down Cake

Quantity: One 9 x 9 inch cake
Oven Temperature: 350° F.
Baking Time: 35 minutes

Ingredients

Cake
1½ cups sifted all-purpose flour
1½ teaspoons double-acting bak-
    ing powder
½ teaspoon salt
¾ cup brown sugar
½ cup butter
2 extra large eggs
½ cup milk
¼ teaspoon nutmeg (optional)
1 tablespoon grated lemon rind

Topping
½ cup brown sugar
2 tablespoons melted butter
9 medium peach halves or 9
    slices of pineapple or 9 me-
    dium plums
9 maraschino cherries (op-
    tional)

Extra
butter for greasing bottom of the
    pan

Procedure

1. In the small mixing bowl combine the ½ cup brown sugar and
2 tablespoons melted butter.
Grease only the bottom of the
cake pan with butter. Arrange the
fruit on the bottom of the pan in
three rows of three. Place a maraschino cherry in the center of
every pineapple slice or in the
center of every peach half. Place
the peach halves cut side down in
the pan. Place the cherries between the plums as illustrated.
With your fingers sprinkle the
brown sugar and butter mixture
evenly over the fruit.

2. Mix the cake following the directions for Salted Peanut Cake. Sift the nutmeg with the flour mixture. Add the lemon rind with the second addition of milk.

3. Watch this cake very carefully while it is baking so the brown sugar on the bottom of the pan does not caramelize. This does not mean you should open the oven door prematurely unless you see or smell that the cake is baking too fast.

4. Allow the cake to cool for 10 minutes. Cut it away from the sides of the pan. Place a serving plate over the top of the pan, and, while holding the plate tightly against the pan, turn the pan over. The cake will fall out.

Jan Wessel's Velvet Cake

Quantity: *One two-layer, 9-inch-diameter cake*
Oven Temperature: *350° F.*
Baking Time: *30 to 40 minutes*

Ingredients
2½ cups cake flour
1 teaspoon baking soda
½ teaspoon salt
1½ cups white sugar
½ cup butter
2 extra large eggs
1 cup buttermilk
1½ teaspoons white vinegar
1 teaspoon vanilla

Extra
1 recipe Fluffy Chocolate Frost-
.ing, page 127
butter for greasing the bottom of
the pan or a waxed paper lining
for the bottom of the pan

Special utensils
two 9-inch-diameter cake pans

Procedure
1. Follow the directions for Salted
Peanut Cake with the following
additions. Beat the butter and
sugar for 10 minutes with the
electric mixer set at high speed.
This will develop the velvet texture of the cake. Add the vanilla
and vinegar with the last addition
of buttermilk. Divide the batter
evenly between two cake pans.
Tap each pan to break any large
air bubbles in the batter. Place
both pans on the center rack of
the oven. The pans should not
touch and must be at least 2
inches from the oven wall. If your
oven is not large enough to allow
this, put one layer on the middle
rack and one on the top rack. Arrange the pans so one is not directly over the other.
2. When the cake has finished
baking, allow it to cool for 10 minutes at room temperature. Carefully loosen each layer from the
sides of the pan with a knife. Invert each pan over a cooling rack
holding the rack against the surface of the cake, and the cake will
easily fall out. Allow the cake to
cool to room temperature on the
rack. Prepare Fluffy Chocolate
Frosting.
3. Transfer one layer top side
down to an attractive serving
plate. Slip pieces of waxed paper
just under the cake all around the
plate to protect the plate from
frosting drips. Brush away all
loose crumbs. With a spatula,
spread the frosting about ¼ inch
thick over the top of the bottom
layer, pushing the frosting almost
to the edge. Spread a thin layer
of frosting around the sides of the
bottom layer. This will keep the
crumbs in place. Carefully position the top layer over the bottom
layer; the top layer should be
right side up. Brush away all
loose crumbs. Spread a thin layer

of frosting over the top and sides of the top layer. Then distribute the balance of the frosting around the top and sides of the cake, making decorative swirls with the spatula. Decorate the cake or leave it plain. Remove the waxed paper before serving.

4. Cut the frosted cake with a sharp, thin-bladed knife. Insert the point of the knife in the center of the cake keeping the point down and the handle up. Slice the cake with an up-and-down motion while pulling the knife toward you. Between cuts, dip the knife blade in warm water and wipe it dry with a cloth.

Fluffy Chocolate Frosting

Quantity: Three cups frosting

Ingredients
5 tablespoons all-purpose flour
1 cup white sugar
1 cup butter
1 cup whole milk
1 teaspoon vanilla
2 1-ounce squares un-
    sweetened chocolate

Special utensil
double boiler

Procedure
1. Plan to have the butter at room temperature when you are ready to begin mixing the frosting.
2. Put the chocolate in the double boiler or heavy saucepan and melt it over a low flame. If you use a saucepan, stir the choco-late constantly to prevent burning. Set the chocolate aside to cool slightly.
3. Measure the flour and put it in a second saucepan. Measure the milk in a glass measuring cup and add 2 tablespoons of milk to the flour. Stir until there are no lumps. Add 2 more tablespoons of milk to the pan and stir; continue gradually adding the milk and stir-ring it to prevent lumps.
4. Place the saucepan over a low flame on the stove and stir con-stantly until the mixture becomes very thick. Remove the pan from the heat and place it in a larger pan of cool water. Cool until mix-ture is lukewarm to the touch. Stirring will hasten the cooling process.
5. Stir in the melted chocolate.
6. Put the butter in a medium mixing bowl and beat it with an electric mixer until it is light and fluffy. Measure the sugar and gradually add it to the butter while continuing the beating process. Add the vanilla and beat for 2 minutes at high speed.
7. Continue beating at high speed while gradually adding the cooled milk and chocolate mixture. Beat until the frosting is light and fluffy with the consistency of whipped cream.

Brownies

Quantity: One 9 x 13 inch pan
Oven Temperature: 350° F.
Baking Time: 30 minutes

Ingredients

- 1 cup all-purpose flour
- 1 teaspoon double-acting baking powder
- ¼ teaspoon salt
- 2 cups white sugar
- ½ cup butter
- 3 extra large eggs
- 4 1-ounce squares unsweetened chocolate
- 1 teaspoon vanilla
- 1 cup chopped walnuts (optional)

Extra

butter for greasing the bottom of the pan
powdered sugar for dusting the top of the cake

Special utensil

double boiler

Procedure

Preparation

1. Read the section introduction.
2. Plan to have all the ingredients at room temperature at the time you are ready to begin, and set out all the ingredients and utensils in a convenient working space.
3. Grease only the bottom of the baking pan with butter.
4. Chop and measure the nuts.

Mixing and baking

1. Preheat the oven to 350°.
2. Fill the bottom pan of the double boiler with water and place it over a medium heat. Place the chocolate in the top of the double boiler and put it over the water to melt. It you use a saucepan, stir the chocolate constantly to prevent burning. Set the chocolate aside to cool slightly.
3. Tear off two pieces of waxed paper approximately 12 inches long. With a metal measuring cup roughly measure out the flour and sift it onto one of the pieces of waxed paper. Move the sifter to the second sheet of waxed paper and measure the flour, baking powder, and salt into the sifter. Pour the excess flour back into the storage container. Run the dry ingredients through the sifter twice, using the waxed paper to catch and transfer them. Set the flour mixture aside.
4. Measure the butter and put it in a medium mixing bowl. Beat it with the electric mixer set on high speed until it is light and fluffy.
5. Gradually beat in the sugar and continue beating for 1 or 2 minutes.
6. Beat the eggs in one at a time. Beat just enough to completely mix the ingredients together.
□ Overbeating at this stage will cause curdling.

7. The chocolate should be cooled to lukewarm. If it isn't, stir it for a few minutes. Stirring will hasten the cooling process.

8. Add the chocolate and vanilla to the butter mixture and stir them in by hand.

9. Sift the flour over the top of the mixture and stir only until all of the ingredients are mixed together.

10. Stir in the chopped nuts.

11. Turn the batter into the cake pan and immediately place it in the center of the middle rack in the oven. Set your timer for 30 minutes.

12. When the timer goes off, test the brownies for doneness by inserting a toothpick in the center of the cake. If the toothpick comes out clean, the brownies are done. If tiny bits of brownie adhere to the toothpick, return the pan to the oven for a few more minutes.

□ Be careful not to overbake the brownies. They will become disappointingly dry.

13. When the brownies are done, place the pan on a cooling rack until it reaches room temperature. While the brownies are still warm, sift powdered sugar over the top.

Gingerbread

Quantity: One 9 x 13 inch pan
Oven Temperature: 350° F.
Baking Time: 30 to 35 minutes

Ingredients

2 cups all-purpose flour
2 teaspoons baking soda
½ teaspoon salt
1 cup brown sugar
1 cup light molasses or Lyle's Golden Syrup
½ cup butter
2 extra large eggs
1 cup buttermilk or sour milk
2 tablespoons unsweetened cocoa
2 teaspoons cinnamon
1½ teaspoons ginger
½ teaspoon nutmeg

Extra

butter for greasing the bottom of the pan
powdered sugar for dusting the top of the cake

Procedure

Preparation

1. Plan to have all the ingredients at room temperature at the time you are ready to begin working and set out all the ingredients and utensils in a convenient working space.

2. Grease only the bottom of the cake pan with butter.

Mixing and baking

1. Preheat the oven to 350°.

2. Tear off two pieces of waxed paper approximately 12 inches long. With a metal measuring cup roughly measure out the flour and sift it onto one of the pieces of waxed paper. Move the sifter to the second sheet of waxed paper and measure the flour, baking soda, salt, cocoa, cinnamon, ginger, and nutmeg into the sifter. Pour the excess flour back into its storage container. Run the dry ingredients through the sifter twice using the waxed paper to catch and transfer them. Set the flour mixture aside.

3. Measure the butter and put it in a medium mixing bowl. Beat it with the electric mixer set on high speed until it is light and fluffy.

4. Gradually beat in the sugar and molasses and continue beating for 1 or 2 minutes.

□ Sift the brown sugar first if it is lumpy.

5. Add the eggs to the butter and sugar mixture. Beat just enough to completely mix the ingredients together.

□ Overbeating at this stage will cause curdling.

6. Measure out the buttermilk in a glass measuring cup. Set it next to the mixer.

7. Add approximately ⅓ of the sifted dry ingredients and beat until the mixture is thoroughly combined. Add ½ of the milk and beat it in. Beat in another ⅓ of the flour and then the rest of the milk. Add the last ⅓ of flour and beat 1 or 2 minutes.

8. Pour the batter immediately into the prepared pan and place it in the center of the middle rack in the oven. Set the timer for 25 minutes.

9. When the timer goes off, test for doneness by inserting a toothpick in the center of the gingerbread. If the toothpick comes out clean, it is done. If tiny bits of gingerbread adhere to the toothpick, return cake to the oven for a few minutes.

10. When the gingerbread is done, place it on the cooling rack until it reaches room temperature. While the gingerbread is still warm, sift powdered sugar over the top.

Air Foam/Butter Base Cakes

This group of cakes is leavened by both air and the chemical leaveners. As indicated by the name, they are mixed using a combination of techniques. An air foam/butter base cake is most often mixed like a butter base cake except the eggs are separated. The egg yolks are mixed in where the whole egg would be. The egg whites are then beaten to the soft peak stage and folded into the batter just before the cake is baked.

The problems that occur in air foam and butter base cakes are also common to this group. It is probably most essential to remember to beat the egg whites with sugar and an acid or cream of tartar for maximum stability. Failure to do this may cause the batter to separate while it is baking, and the finished cake will have an undesirable layered texture.

Pound Cake

Quantity: Three 9 x 5 inch cakes
Oven Temperature: 350° F.
Baking Time: 50 minutes

Ingredients
4½ cups cake flour
1 tablespoon double-acting baking powder
½ teaspoon salt
2⅓ cups superfine white sugar
1 cup butter
8 extra large egg whites
6 extra large egg yolks
1 cup milk
1 teaspoon cream of tartar

Optional flavoring: use only one
1 tablespoon rose water
2 tablespoons vanilla
3 tablespoons brandy
3 tablespoons lemon juice + 1 tablespoon grated lemon rind

Extra
butter for greasing the bottom of the pans
powdered sugar for dusting the tops of the cakes

Utensils
glass measuring cup
set of graduated metal measuring cups
set of measuring spoons
2 medium mixing bowls
3 small mixing bowls
flour sifter
electric mixer
rubber scraper
spatula or wire whisk
grater
3 standard bread pans
waxed paper
kitchen timer
2 cooling racks
toothpick
hot pad

Procedure

Preparation
1. Read the section introduction.
2. One hour before the time you have set aside to mix a pound cake, remove the eggs from the refrigerator. Separate them while they are cold. For this you will need 3 small bowls, all of them clean and grease free. Crack the first egg and split it in half over one of the bowls. Some of the white will drop in the bowl immediately. Hold the yolk in half of the shell, and, by transferring it back and forth from shell to shell, drain out the rest of the white. Drop the yolk into the second empty bowl, and with your finger, scrape out any white still remaining in the shells. Pour each yolk-free white into the third bowl. Set both bowls aside until the eggs reach room temperature.
□ Never put egg whites in a plastic bowl.
□ The egg white should be completely free of any traces of the fat-containing egg yolk. Remove any specks of egg yolk from the white with a piece of broken eggshell.
□ If by some misfortune the egg yolk breaks and spills completely into the white, transfer this egg to a storage container and refrigerate it for future use in a whole egg mixture. Wash out the bowl and begin again.
3. Plan to have all the ingredients at room temperature at the time you are ready to begin, and set out all the ingredients and utensils in a convenient working space.

4. If you wish to use lemon flavoring, grate the peel and squeeze the lemon juice.

5. Grease only the bottoms of the loaf pans with butter.

Mixing and baking

1. Preheat the oven to 350°

2. Tear off two pieces of waxed paper approximately 12 inches long. With a metal measuring cup roughly measure out the flour and sift it onto one of the pieces of waxed paper. Move the sifter to the second sheet of waxed paper and measure the flour, baking powder, and salt into the sifter. Pour the excess flour back into its storage container. Run the dry ingredients through the sifter twice using the waxed paper to catch and transfer them. Set the flour mixture aside.

3. Measure the butter and put it in a medium mixing bowl. Beat it with the electric mixer until it is light and fluffy.

4. Gradually beat in 1⅓ cups of the sugar and continue beating for 1 or 2 minutes.

5. Gradually add the egg yolks to the butter and sugar mixture. Beat just enough to completely mix the ingredients together.

□ Overbeating at this stage will cause curdling.

6. Measure out the milk in a glass measuring cup. Set it next to the mixer.

7. Add approximately ⅓ of the sifted dry ingredients and beat until the mixture is thoroughly combined. Add ½ of the milk and whichever flavoring you choose to use, and beat them in. Beat in the second ⅓ of the flour and then the rest of the milk. Add the last ⅓ of flour and beat for 1 or 2 minutes. Set the bowl aside and wash the beaters.

8. Pour the egg whites into a deep grease-free, straight-sided bowl. Measure out the remaining cup of sugar and set it next to the electric mixer with the cream of tartar and measuring spoons.

9. Begin beating the egg whites with your electric mixer set on high speed. In a short time large air bubbles will form on the top of the egg whites, while some liquid remains on the bottom of the bowl. The egg whites should still be fluid and transparent. Stop the mixer for a minute and measure and add the cream of tartar and 2 or 3 tablespoons of the previously measured 1 cup of sugar to the egg whites. Turn the mixer on to high and continue beating while adding the balance of the sugar tablespoon by tablespoon.

□ Don't dump the sugar in all at once. You must add it gradually to the egg whites.

10. In 1 or 2 minutes stop the mixer and pull out the beaters. The egg whites should have reached the soft peak stage by now. The bubbles should be getting smaller and the foam white. As you remove the beaters the egg white that follows the beaters out of the mixture will bend over in soft curls.

11. Remove the egg whites from the mixer as soon as the soft peak stage is reached and do the following immediately. Gently fold about 1 cup of the batter into the egg whites. Folding is accomplished by cutting through the egg whites, lifting up a portion of them, and turning this over. Repeat this motion four or five times, turning the bowl slightly each time.

□ The whites will rapidly lose their volume if they are allowed to stand.

12. Now add the balance of the batter to the egg white mixture. Continue folding and rotating the bowl until the mixture is an even color.

13. Use a measuring cup to distribute the batter evenly among the loaf pans. Each pan should be filled half way. Cut through the batter in each pan in each direction to break up any large air bubbles.

14. Immediately place the cake pans on the middle rack of the oven. The pans should be 2 inches apart and 2 inches from the oven walls. Set your timer for 50 minutes. Do not open the oven door until the timer goes off.

15. When the timer goes off, test the cakes for doneness by inserting a toothpick in the center of each cake. If the toothpick comes out clean, the cake is done. If tiny bits of cake adhere to the toothpick, return the cake to the oven for a few minutes.

16. When the cakes are done, cool them in the pans for 15 minutes. Carefully loosen each cake from the sides of the pan with a knife and turn them out of the pans onto cooling racks. Dust the top of each cake with powdered sugar. This is easily accomplished if you put the powdered sugar in your sifter and sift the sugar over the cakes.

17. Wrap the cakes tightly in plastic and store them in the freezer for future use.

□ Remove all excess air from the plastic bags and seal them well to prevent frostbite.

Fern Evans Kruecke's Chocolate Cake

Quantity: One 9 x 13 inch cake
Oven Temperature: 325° F.
Baking Time: 50 to 55 minutes

Ingredients
2½ cups cake flour
1½ teaspoons double-acting bak-
    ing powder
½ teaspoon baking soda
¼ teaspoon salt
2 cups white sugar
¾ cup butter
3 extra large eggs
1 cup buttermilk
1 teaspoon cream of tartar
3 1-ounce squares of un-
    sweetened chocolate
1 teaspoon vanilla

Extra
1 recipe Mocha Chocolate Frost-
    ing, page 136
butter for greasing the bottom of
    the pan or a waxed paper lining
    for the bottom of the pan
extra whole nuts for decoration

Special utensils
double boiler
9 x 13 inch cake pan

Procedure
1. Preheat the oven to 325°.
2. Follow the directions for Pound
Cake through Mixing and baking
Step 12. Melt the chocolate in a
double boiler or over a low flame
in a heavy saucepan, stirring constantly to prevent it from burning.

Remove the pan from the stove
and set it aside to cool slightly.
Beat the cooled chocolate into
the egg yolk, butter, and sugar
mixture (mixing and baking Step
5) in three or four additions.
3. Turn the batter into the cake
pan and immediately place the
cake pan in the center of the top
rack in the oven. Set your timer
for 50 minutes. Do not open the
oven door until the timer goes off.
4. When the timer goes off, test
the cake for doneness by inserting a toothpick in the center
of the cake. If the toothpick
comes out clean, the cake is
done. If tiny bits of cake adhere
to the toothpick, return the cake
to the oven for a few minutes.
5. When the cake has finished
baking, allow it to cool for 15 minutes at room temperature while
preparing Mocha Chocolate Frosting.
6. Spread the frosting evenly over
the top of the cooled cake. Decorate with the extra nuts.
7. Refrigerate the cake, because
the frosting is made with custard
base.
8. Cut the frosted cake with a
sharp thin-bladed knife. Hold the
point down and the handle up
and slice the cake with an up-
and-down motion while pulling
the knife toward you. Dip the
knife blade in warm water occasionally and wipe it dry with a
cloth.

Mocha Chocolate Frosting

Quantity: Two and one-half cups frosting

Ingredients

2 tablespoons all-purpose flour
⅛ teaspoon salt
2 cups powdered sugar
1 tablespoon soft butter
1 extra large egg yolk
¾ cup milk
3 1-ounce squares of un-
    sweetened chocolate
2 teaspoons vanilla
2 tablespoons strong coffee
1 cup broken walnuts

Procedure

1. Measure out the milk in a glass measuring cup. Measure the flour and put it in a heavy saucepan. Add the milk 2 or 3 tablespoons at a time, stirring in each addition of milk so there are no lumps. Cook the mixture over a low flame, stirring constantly, until it is thickened. Remove the pan from the heat.

2. Beat the egg yolk slightly with a fork and add 1 tablespoon of the flour-milk mixture and beat them together. Add 2 more table-spoons of the flour-milk mixture and beat. Now add the egg yolk mixture to the saucepan containing the flour-milk mixture. Stir until blended. Return the pan to a low heat and cook for 5 minutes, stirring constantly. Remove from the heat.

3. Cut the squares of chocolate into quarters and drop them in the pan. Stir the mixture until the chocolate is completely melted. Measure the butter and add it to the mixture in the pan. Stir to blend in the butter.

4. Scrape the cooked mixture out of the pan into a medium mixing bowl. Measure out and combine the powdered sugar and salt, and sift 1 cup of the powdered sugar over the mixture in the bowl. Beat with the electric mixer until the sugar is completely blended in. Sift the second cup of sugar over the mixture. Measure and add the vanilla and coffee. Beat with the electric mixer until the frosting is very smooth. Stir in the broken nuts with a wooden spoon.

Cookies

Cookies are probably the most popular group of recipes included in this book. A cook who would never attempt to bake a cake or soufflé almost certainly has made a batch of cookies at least once.

Cookies have much to recommend them. They are simple to make, and they are easily stored and transported. They are a favorite snack of children, a pleasing accompaniment to a lunch, tea, or dinner, and in general a pacifier for almost everyone's sweet tooth.

Perhaps cookies are most important in their relationship to holidays. In this country the word cookie almost belongs to Christmas. Most of the cultures that compose our rich ethnic origins bake some kind of special cookie to celebrate the winter holidays. We think these cookies are a marvelous, sentimental tradition for a variety of reasons. They preserve our heritage. They bring happiness to children, and homeliness to a house. They give the baker an opportunity to express his creative abilities as well as to demonstrate his excellence as a cook.

There is a great deal of enjoyment and satisfaction to be had from baking and decorating a beautiful assortment of cookies and serving them with a special holiday meal. And, finally, a box of cookies, with its very personal touch, is a thoughtful present for friends.

The word cookie is thought to be derived from the Dutch word *koekje,* which is the diminutive of *koek,* or cake. Cookies are, in fact, very short sweet cakes. They are mixed using the same procedures used for conventional cakes. The main difference is in the proportions of ingredients used. Cookie dough is richer, containing more fat. The dough is usually very stiff and has little, if any, extra liquid. Conventional cakes, on the other hand, contain less fat and a higher ratio of liquid to the other ingredients. As a result, they have a very fluid dough or batter.

The main pitfall in making successful cookies lies in the baking. Correct oven temperature and the even circulation of heat are critical factors in producing well-shaped and browned cookies. Good quality baking sheets are essential. Thin, inexpensive, or old and blackened sheets will not conduct heat properly. You must use a heavy metal cookie sheet with a shiny top surface and a dull underside for the best results. You must never bake cookies on more than 1 oven rack at a time. The circulation of heat in the oven is seriously affected when one baking sheet is placed over another in the oven.

Cookies may be grouped into four general categories. These are:

Drop cookies: The dough for these cookies requires no shaping. It is dropped on the baking sheet in mounds and baked as is.

Rolled cookies: The dough for these cookies is chilled and rolled out like a pie crust. It is then cut out with special cookie cutters.

Pressed and shaped cookies: The dough for these cookies is forced through a special press, formed in a mold, or rolled and shaped with the hands.

Pan or bar cookies: The dough for these cookies is pressed into a cake pan and usually covered with some kind of topping. The cookies are cut into bars after they are baked.

Basic Cookies

Quantity: *Four dozen 2-inch cookies*
Oven Temperature: *375° F.*
Baking Time: *8 to 10 minutes*

Ingredients

3 cups all-purpose flour
1 teaspoon double-acting baking powder
⅛ teaspoon salt
1 cup sugar (this could be all white, all brown, or ½ white and ½ brown)
1 cup butter
1 extra large egg
2 tablespoons cream (light or heavy)
1 teaspoon vanilla

Flavoring
Add any entry. Do not overflavor your cookies by adding more than one entry:
¼ teaspoon mace or nutmeg
1 teaspoon cinnamon
1 tablespoon grated lemon rind
1 tablespoon grated orange rind
1 cup uncooked oatmeal
1 cup uncooked oatmeal + 1 tablespoon lemon orange rind
1½ cups broken nuts
1½ cups raisins
2 cups chocolate chips
½ cup chocolate chips + ½ cup raisins + ½ cup broken nuts
1 cup chocolate chips + ½ cup broken nuts

Extra

butter for greasing the cookie sheets
jam, nuts, chocolate chips, raisins, flavored sugars (page 62), baker's decorations, colored egg glaze for decorating the cookies

Utensils

set of graduated metal measuring cups
set of measuring spoons
large mixing bowl
flour sifter
electric mixer
rubber scraper
spatula
2 cookie sheets
2 cooling racks
waxed paper
paper towels
kitchen timer
hot pad
airtight storage container

Utensils for flavoring and decorations
small bowls for mixing sugars and egg glaze
hand grater
French knife
small soft brushes
cookie cutters
rolling pin
pastry cloth and rolling pin sleeve
flat-bottomed glass with 3-inch-diameter nut grinder

◻ We have baked countless varieties of cookies, each of them special in one way or another. But this recipe stands out as the most versatile, lovely cookie dough. It can take on different flavors and shapes and always is easy to work with. We have suggested many possible flavor additions under the basic ingredients list. Cookies mixed with chocolate chips, raisins, oatmeal, or nuts in the dough should be baked as drop cookies. The flavored cookies may be rolled out and cut out with cookie cutters or formed into balls and pressed flat on the cookie sheets. The illustrations will help stimulate your imagination about countless forms this basic cookie dough can assume and special ways to decorate them.

Procedure

Preparation
1. Read the chapter introduction.
2. Plan to have all the ingredients at room temperature at the time you are ready to begin working, and set out all the ingredients and utensils in a convenient working space.

Mixing
1. Tear off two pieces of waxed paper approximately 12 inches long. With a metal measuring cup roughly measure out the flour and sift it onto one of the pieces of waxed paper. Move the sifter to the second sheet of waxed paper and measure the flour, baking powder, and salt into the sifter. Pour the excess flour back into its storage container. Run the dry ingredients through the sifter twice using the waxed paper to catch and transfer them. Set the flour mixture aside.
2. Measure the butter and put it in a large mixing bowl. Beat it with the electric mixer until it is light and fluffy.
3. Gradually beat in the sugar and continue beating for 1 or 2 minutes.
□ If you use brown sugar, be sure to sift the lumps out before adding the sugar to the butter.
4. Add the egg to the butter and sugar mixture. Beat just enough to completely mix the ingredients together.
□ Overbeating at this stage will cause curdling.
5. Measure out the vanilla or other flavorings and cream. Beat them into the mixture.

6. Add approximately ⅓ of the sifted dry ingredients and beat until they are thoroughly combined. Add a second ⅓ of the dry ingredients and beat until combined. Repeat with last ⅓ of the dry ingredients.

7. With a wooden spoon stir in any lumpy additions to the cookie dough. These would include chocolate chips, raisins, nuts, and oatmeal.
8. Cover the bowl with waxed paper or plastic wrap and place it in the refrigerator for 2 hours.

Rolling and shaping
Turn the oven on to 375° and lightly grease the cookie sheets with butter.

Drop Cookies
1. Remove the chilled dough from the refrigerator. Scoop out small pieces of dough from the bowl with a teaspoon. Arrange them on the greased cookie sheet leaving 3 inches of space between each ball. When the cookie sheet is filled, return the unused dough to the refrigerator.
2. Place the cookie sheet on the top rack of the oven. If two cookie sheets will fit on the top rack, it is

all right to bake them both at the same time. Remember the edges of either cookie sheet must be 2 inches from the oven walls. Set the timer and bake.

□ Never bake cookies in pans with high sides. The sides block the heat circulation. Turn these pans over and bake the cookies on the bottom.

□ Watch the first batch of cookies carefully. If they are browning too quickly, reduce the oven temperature 25°. If the cookies at one end of the sheet are browning faster, rotate the sheets halfway through the baking time. If the bottoms brown too quickly, and you have reduced the oven heat, you may try placing the cookie sheets under the broiler 5 to 6 inches from the heat for 1 or 2 minutes. Be careful!

3. Allow cookies to cool and firm up for 1 or 2 minutes after they are removed from the oven. Carefully loosen the cookies with a spatula and transfer them to the cooling racks. When the cookies have cooled, transfer them to a serving plate or an airtight storage container.

4. Repeat shaping and baking the rest of the dough. Wipe the

cookie sheet with a clean paper towel after every batch. Cool the cookie sheet before placing a new batch of cookies on it.

□ If you do not have enough dough to completely fill out the last cookie sheet, bake these cookies on the bottom of a smaller cake or pie pan. When only one area of a cookie sheet is filled, the heat is attracted to this area, causing the cookies to brown very quickly on the bottoms and consequently to burn.

□ If, by accident, you burn the bottoms of a batch of cookies, scrape the burned area away with a hand grater.

Rolled Cookies
1. Divide the chilled dough into four equal parts. Use a knife or spatula to mark and separate it. Remove one part of dough from the bowl, pat it into a smooth round shape and place it in the center of the prepared pastry cloth (see page 98). Return the rest of the dough to the refrigerator. Cover the rolling pin with the sleeve. Roll out the dough with quick light strokes that begin in the center of the dough. Roll toward the edges in all directions lifting the rolling pin slightly as you reach the edge. This action will prevent the edges of the dough from cracking and splitting. Adjust the direction of the rolling pin to keep the dough as close to a perfect circle as possible.

□ If the dough sticks, sprinkle it lightly with flour.
2. Roll the dough to a uniform thickness of ⅛ inch.
3. Dip your cookie cutters into some flour and with a firm even pressure cut the cookies out. Transfer them to the greased

cookie sheets with a spatula, leaving 1 inch of space all around each cookie. Decorate the cookies at this time. If you wish to paint designs on them, beat 1 egg yolk with ¼ teaspoon of water and add a few drops of food coloring. Apply the colored glaze with a soft brush.

□ Do not leave any open spaces on the cookie sheets. Fill them completely.

□ Use a high quality brush which will not lose its bristles on the cookies.

4. Proceed as directed from Step 2 of Drop Cookies.

□ The cookie dough will toughen every time you reroll it because the rolling process develops the gluten structure in the flour. You might consider cutting the scraps into smaller pieces and baking them as is.

Pressed Cookies

1. Remove the chilled dough from the refrigerator. Scoop out small pieces of dough from the bowl with a teaspoon. Lightly flour your hands and roll the dough lightly between your palms making small walnut-size balls.

2. Arrange the balls on the greased cookie sheets leaving 3 inches of space around every ball. Flour the bottom of a glass and evenly press down on each ball of dough until it is ⅛ inch thick. Dip the bottom of the glass into flour before you press down each cookie.

3. Decorate the cookies at this time. If you wish to paint designs on them, beat 1 egg yolk with ¼ teaspoon of water and add a few drops of food coloring. Apply the colored glaze with a soft brush.

4. Proceed as directed from Step 2 of Drop Cookies.

Chocolate Oatmeal Cookies

Quantity: Eight dozen 1-inch cookies
Oven Temperature: 350° F.
Baking Time: 8 to 10 minutes

Ingredients
2 cups all-purpose flour
3 cups uncooked oatmeal
2 teaspoons double-acting baking powder
1 teaspoon salt
2 cups white sugar
1 cup butter
2 extra large eggs
4 1-ounce squares un-
   sweetened chocolate
3 teaspoons vanilla

Extra
butter for greasing the cookie
   sheet

Special utensil
double boiler

Procedure
Follow the directions for Basic Cookies. Melt the chocolate in a double boiler or over a low flame in a heavy pan, stirring constantly. Set the pan containing the melted chocolate in a slightly larger pan or bowl of cold water to cool it slightly. Beat the cooled choco-late into the batter just before adding the flour. Shape following the instructions given for Drop Cookies.

Snickerdoodle Cookies

Quantity: Five and three-fourths dozen 2-inch cookies
Oven Temperature: 400° F.
Baking Time: 10 minutes

Ingredients

Cookie Dough
2¾ cups all-purpose flour
1 tablespoon double-acting
   baking powder
½ teaspoon salt
1½ cups white sugar
1 cup butter
2 extra large eggs

Roll Dough in
4 tablespoons white sugar
1 tablespoon cinnamon, ½ teaspoon nutmeg

Extra
butter for greasing the cookie
   sheets

Procedure
Follow the directions for Basic Cookies. Shape as Pressed Cook-ies. Before placing balls of dough on the cookie sheets, roll them in the sugar and spice mixture. Cookies may be pressed flat with a glass or baked in ball shapes.

Pecan Finger Cookies

Quantity: *Three and one-half dozen 1½-inch cookies*
Oven Temperature: *325° F.*
Baking Time: *18 minutes*

Ingredients

2 cups all-purpose flour
½ teaspoon salt
½ powdered sugar
1 cup butter
1 tablespoon cold water
1 teaspoon vanilla
1½ cups broken pecans

Extra

butter for greasing the cookie sheets
powdered sugar for dusting the tops of the cookies

Procedure

Follow the directions for Basic Cookies. If the powdered sugar is caked, sift it before measuring. Chop the pecans coarsely with a French knife. Shape the cookie dough into oblong fingers, 1½ inches long. Don't flatten the cookies. While the cookies are cooling on the racks, dust them with powdered sugar. This is easily accomplished if you put ¼ cup of powdered sugar in your flour sifter and sift the sugar over the cookies.

Peanut Butter Cookies

Quantity: *Four and one-half dozen ½-inch cookies*
Oven Temperature: *350° F.*
Baking Time: *12 to 15 minutes*

Ingredients

1¾ cups all-purpose flour
2½ teaspoons double-acting baking powder
½ teaspoon salt
½ cup white sugar
½ cup brown sugar
¾ cup butter or margarine
1 extra large egg
½ cup peanut butter

Extra

butter for greasing the cookie sheets

Procedure

Follow the directions for Basic Cookies. Treat the peanut butter as a fat, beating it with the butter before adding the sugar. Shape as Pressed Cookies. Flatten the little balls with the floured tines of a fork instead of a glass.

Pinwheel Cookies

Quantity: Eleven dozen 1-inch
cookies
Oven Temperature: 400° F.
Baking Time: 5 minutes

Ingredients
  3 cups all-purpose flour
  1 teaspoon double-acting bak-
    ing powder
  ½ teaspoon salt
1¾ cups white sugar
  1 cup butter
  2 extra large egg yolks
  ⅓ cup milk
  2 1-ounce squares un-
    sweetened chocolate

Extra
butter for greasing the cookie
  sheets
1 egg white beaten with 1 teaspoon water to coat layers of
  dough

Special utensil
double boiler

Procedure
1. Follow the directions for Basic
Cookies. Melt the chocolate in a
double boiler or in a heavy pan
over a low flame, stirring constantly. Set the pan containing the
melted chocolate in a slightly
larger pan or bowl of cold water
to cool it slightly. Divide the
dough into two slightly unequal
portions. Place the smaller portion
of dough in the small mixing
bowl, and with the electric mixer
or a wooden spoon, work the
cooled chocolate into the dough
until it is no longer visible as a
separate ingredient.
2. Read the directions for Rolled
Cookies. Roll the natural-colored
dough out on a pastry cloth in an

oblong shape. The dough should
be ⅛ inch thick. Tear off a piece
of waxed paper and place it over
the rolled-out dough. Carefully
turn the pastry cloth, dough, and
waxed paper sandwich over. Use
a small cutting board to hold the
sandwich rigid. Without tearing
the dough peel off the pastry
cloth. Set the natural dough and
waxed paper aside.

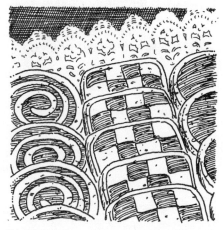

3. Roll out the chocolate-colored
dough to the same thickness
and shape as the natural dough.

145

Transfer the chocolate dough to a sheet of waxed paper. Brush the top surface of the natural dough with a pastry brush and 1 egg white beaten with 1 teaspoon water.

4. Lay the chocolate dough on the natural dough and peel the waxed paper off. Roll as illustrated, pressing the two layers of dough together as you roll them.

Wrap the roll of dough in waxed paper and chill it in the refrigerator for 1 hour.

5. Slice the dough with a sharp thin-bladed knife as soon as you remove it from the refrigerator. The slices should be ⅛ inch thick. Arrange the cookie slices on the cookie sheets leaving 1 inch of space around each cookie.

Molasses Cookies

Quantity: Five dozen 2-inch cookies
Oven Temperature: 375° F.
Baking Time: 12 minutes

Extra
butter for greasing the cookie sheets
coarse sugar to sprinkle on top of the cookies

Ingredients
4 cups all-purpose flour
2½ teaspoons double-acting baking soda
1 teaspoon salt
1 cup white sugar
1 cup light molasses
1 cup butter or margarine
3 extra large eggs
1 tablespoon white vinegar
1 tablespoon grated orange rind
1½ cups raisins

Procedure
Follow the directions for Basic Cookies. Add the molasses, vinegar, and orange rind after the eggs are beaten in. Stir in the raisins after the dry ingredients have been added.

□ Shape as Pressed Cookies. Dip one side of the dough balls into the coarse sugar and place this side up on the cookie sheet. The pressure of the glass will embed the sugar in the dough.

Joyce Kaye's Ginger Cookies

Quantity: *Three dozen 5½-inch gingerbread men*
Oven Temperature: *350° F.*
Baking Time: *10 minutes*

Ingredients

3¼ cups all-purpose flour
  2 teaspoons double-acting baking soda
  ⅛ teaspoon salt
1½ cups white sugar
  2 tablespoons dark corn syrup
  1 cup butter
  1 extra large egg
  1 tablespoon water
  2 tablespoons grated orange rind
  2 teaspoons cinnamon
  1 teaspoon ginger

Extra

butter for greasing the cookie sheets
currants for decoration

Procedure

Follow the directions for Basic Cookies. Add the corn syrup, orange rind, cinnamon, ginger, and water after beating in the egg. Shape as Rolled Cookies.
□ This dough is perfect for gingerbread men.

Jam Squares

Quantity: *Eight dozen 1-inch cookie squares*
Oven Temperature: *350° F.*
Baking Time: *35 minutes*

Ingredients
1½ cups sifted all-purpose flour
1½ cups oatmeal
  1 teaspoon double-acting bak-
     ing powder
¼ teaspoon salt
  1 cup brown sugar
¾ cup butter
  1 12-ounce jar of apricot jam or
     raspberry jam or orange
     marmalade

Extra
butter for greasing the cake pan

Special utensil
One 9 x 9 inch pan

Procedure
Follow the directions for Basic
Cookies. After the dough has
chilled slightly, divide it into two
equal parts. Using your fingers,
press ½ the dough into the bot-

tom of a lightly greased 9 x 9 inch
pan. Spread the dough evenly
leaving no uncovered areas on
the bottom of the pan. Spread the
jar of jam or marmalade evenly
over the dough. With your fingers
crumble the balance of the dough
on top of the jam layer. Spread
the crumbled dough as evenly as
possible. Set timer and bake. Cool
for 10 minutes before cutting the
pan of cookies into individual
squares and removing them to
cooling racks.

Toffee Squares

Quantity: Six dozen 1-inch cookie
   squares
Oven Temperature: 350° F.
Baking Time: 25 minutes

Ingredients
  2 cups all-purpose flour
  ½ teaspoon salt
  1 cup dark brown sugar
  1 cup butter
  1 extra large egg
  1 4-ounce bar of German choc-
     olate (found in baking sec-
     tion of most supermarkets)
  ¾ cup salted roasted almonds

Extra
butter for greasing the cake pan

Special utensils
double boiler
one 9 x 13 inch pan

Procedure
1. Follow the directions for Basic
Cookies. Using your fingers, press
the dough into the bottom of a 9
x 13 inch pan. This should be
done evenly with no areas of pan
left uncovered. Set the timer and
bake the dough.
2. While the dough is baking,
melt the chocolate in a double
boiler or in a heavy pan over a
low flame, stirring constantly.
When the chocolate is completely
melted, remove the pan from the
stove. Using a nut grinder or a
French knife, chop the almonds to
pieces the size of grains of barley.
3. Spread the melted chocolate
over the dough as soon as you
take it out of the oven. Smooth
the chocolate with your spatula.
Sprinkle the chopped nuts evenly
over the chocolate. Cool at room
temperature until the chocolate
is firm but still slightly soft to the
touch. Cut the pan of cookies into
individual squares and remove
them to cooling racks.
□ If the chocolate sticks to the
knife, dip the knife in a glass of
cold water before each cut.

Dream Bars

Quantity: Eighty-one 1-inch
  cookie squares
Oven Temperature: 375° F.
Baking Time: 25 to 30 minutes

Ingredients

Cookie base
  1 cup all-purpose flour
  ½ cup butter
  ½ cup brown sugar

Topping
  2 tablespoons all-purpose flour
  ½ teaspoon double-acting bak-
    ing powder
  ¼ teaspoon salt
  1 cup brown sugar
  2 extra large eggs
  1 teaspoon vanilla
  1½ cups shredded coconut
  1 cup chopped nuts

Special utensil
one 9 x 9 inch pan

Procedure

1. Follow the directions for Basic
Cookies. Using your fingers, press
the cookie base dough into the
bottom of a 9 x 9 inch pan. This
should be done evenly with no
areas of the pan left uncovered.
2. For the topping, beat the eggs,
until they are a light lemon color.
Beat in the brown sugar and then
the flour, baking powder, and salt.
Add the vanilla and beat this mixture until it is smooth. With a
wooden spoon stir in the coconut
and chopped nuts. Spread the
topping evenly over the cookie
base.
3. Set timer and bake. Cool for 10
minutes before cutting the pan of
cookies into individual squares
and removing them to a cooling
rack.

Jellies and Jams

There is a special magic in making your own jelly or jam. First there is the challenge of finding the fresh fruit. Then there is the wonderful smell of the fruit cooking in your kitchen, and later the reassuring pop of the lids as they seal on the jars. Finally, the beautifully colored jelly jars lined up on your kitchen shelf are enough to make any cook burst with pride.

Jelly is made from cooking equal amounts of strained fruit juice and sugar until a chemical change occurs which causes them to jell into a crystal clear substance. Jam is made from fruit pulp and sugar cooked until they combine into a semi-solid opaque substance. Jelly or jam made with natural fruit pectin has a fragile and tender consistency totally unlike fruit made with added commercial pectin.

Natural fruit pectin deteriorates rapidly after the fruit is picked. To make jelly or jam successfully, you must have a fresh, abundant supply of fruit. You may grow it yourself, hunt for it growing wild in the countryside, visit a ranch or farm to purchase it, or buy it on an early morning trip to a big city produce market. Don't attempt to buy the fruit at a local market. The cost is usually prohibitive for the quantities of fruit you will need, and there is no absolute guarantee of the freshness.

For best results, the fruit should have a good color and flavor. Choose some fruit that is just ripe and some that is slightly underripe. Avoid bruised or damaged fruit.

Jelly

Quantity: *Four ½-pint jars of jelly*

Ingredients
4 cups strained hot fruit juice
4 cups white sugar
water

Suggested fruits
Concord grapes, boysenberries,
blackberries, currants, crab apples, quince, tart apples, sour
cherries

Utensils
glass measuring cup
set of graduated metal measuring
cups
large metal spoon
ladle (optional)
medium mixing bowl
colander
jelly kettle, 8-to-10-quart capacity
with a broad, flat bottom and
high sides
large-size kettle
2 clean kitchen towels
cheesecloth or jelly bag made
from two or three thicknesses
of fine cheesecloth stitched together to make a bag 10 x 12
inches with one open end
kitchen thermometer
paring knife
kitchen tongs
4 ½-pint mason jars
new lids and bands or paraffin
gummed labels
2 large hot pads

Procedure
1. Read the chapter introduction.
2. Set out all the utensils in a
convenient working space.
3. Spread out one of the towels
on a level counter in an out-of-
the-way area of the kitchen.
4. Carefully examine the rims of
the mason jars for chips. Save
any chipped jars for uses other
than canning.
□ Jars with chipped rims will not
seal properly.
5. Wash the mason jars in very
hot soapy water. Rinse them well.
Fill each jar with hot tap water
and place it in the large kettle.
Fill the kettle with enough hot
water to completely cover the
jars. Cover it and put it on the
stove over high heat. When the
water comes to a full boil, turn
the heat to low and allow the jars
to stand in the hot water until you
are ready to use them. Separate
the lids and drop them in the hot
water.
6. To determine the temperature
required to jell your fruit, you
must know the temperature at
which water boils on the day
you make your jelly. The boiling
point of water is affected by alti-
tude and atmospheric conditions.
Bring a kettle of water to boil. Use
your kitchen thermometer to determine the exact temperature at
which the water boiled. For
an accurate reading, hold the
thermometer in a vertical position
with the bulb completely covered
by the water, but not touching the
bottom of the kettle.
7. Wash the fruit carefully. Discard all spoiled or bruised pieces.
Remove the stem and blossom
ends from the fruit. Do not remove the peel or core from the
fruit. Both contain pectin. If the
fruit is large, cut it into small
pieces. Wash berries carefully
without mashing them. Lift them
from the wash water. The dirt will
be left behind in the water.
8. Place the cleaned fruit in the
jelly kettle. For hard fruits (apples

or quince) add enough cold water to just cover the fruit pieces. For soft fruits (berries or grapes) add ¼ cup of water for every 2 cups of fruit. Crush the soft fruit against the sides of the pan.

9. Place the kettle on the stove over the highest heat. You must never leave the jelly kettle while it is on the stove. Give the fruit all of your attention. Stir the fruit every few minutes to prevent it from sticking to the bottom of the kettle and burning. As you stir, smash the fruit against the sides of the kettle to release the juice. Cook soft fruits about 10 minutes and hard fruits about 20 minutes or until soft.

□ Do not stir the fruit either vigorously or continuously. Stirring will lower the temperature of the fruit in the kettle. To maximize the benefits from the natural fruit pectin, the fruit should be heated to a very high temperature in a short time.

10. Remove the kettle from the heat. Wet the jelly bag with hot tap water and squeeze out the excess water. Place the jelly bag inside the colander and the colander inside the mixing bowl. (If you don't have a jelly bag, line the inside of the colander with three layers of cheesecloth. All edges of the cheesecloth must hang over the sides of the colander.) Pour the hot fruit pulp and juice into the jelly bag. Allow the liquid to drain through the bag for about 10 minutes. Do not squeeze the bag.

□ If you squeeze the bag, fine pieces of fruit pulp will ooze through and your jelly won't be crystal clear.

11. Rinse out the kettle. Measure the hot strained juice in a glass

measuring cup. Pour 4 cups of juice back in to the jelly kettle and set the rest aside. Add 1 cup of sugar for every cup of juice (4 cups sugar) and stir until the sugar is dissolved.

□ Never cook more than 4 cups of fruit juice at one time. You may cook less than 4 cups.

□ Cook the remaining juice after you finish the first batch.

12. Place the kettle back on the stove over the highest heat. You must not leave the kettle unattended. Stir the fruit juice once every minute to prevent caramelization and burning of the sugar on the bottom of the pan. After a few minutes the fruit will foam up and rise to the top of the kettle. Do not turn the heat down when this happens. Before the fruit juice reaches the correct temperature for jelling to occur, it must boil like this. Now begin testing for jelly with either the spoon test or a kitchen thermometer.

Spoon test
Dip a cold metal spoon into the boiling jelly, and when two drops come together and sheet off the spoon and the jelly drops off the spoon in a sheet instead of individual drops, the jelly is done.

Thermometer test
Hold the thermometer in a vertical position and insert it in the boiling liquid far enough to completely cover the bulb, but not far enough to touch the bottom of the kettle. (A thermometer held against the bottom of the kettle will not accurately read the temperature of the liquid inside the kettle.) When the thermometer shows a reading equal to the boiling point of water you determined earlier plus 8°, the jelly is done.

13. Remove the pan from the stove. Stir the jelly down and skim the white foam off the top with the spoon. Set the kettle aside momentarily. You must work quickly. Both the jelly and the mason jars must be boiling hot to seal safely and correctly.

14. Remove the jars from the kettle of water with the kitchen tongs. Turn them upside down to drain for a few seconds on the clean towel. Then, turn them right side up. Holding the kettle close to the mouth of the jar, pour the jelly into each jar. If it is easier for you, put the jelly into the jars with a sterilized ladle. Again, hold the ladle close to the jar. Fill each jar to ⅛ inch from the rim. Pour any extra jelly into a cup or glass.
□ Unwanted air bubbles may form if the jelly drops a long distance into the jars.
15. Dampen the second towel and wipe any spills from the rims and threads of the jars. Remove the lids from the water with the kitchen tongs and put 1 on each jar. The rubber ringed side of the lid lies against the rim of the

glass. Screw a band on each jar. Using hot pad, tighten each band. Invert the jars for a few seconds to kill any bacteria on the lid. Allow the jars to stand undisturbed until they cool to room temperature. This will take about 12 hours.
16. As the jars cool you will hear a loud pop come from each one. Each pop will come at a different time. This noise is caused by the vacuum formed inside the jar and means the jar is safely sealed. When the jars are cooled, each lid should be indented in the center. If it is not, the jar has not sealed and must be stored in the refrigerator and used immediately.
17. Label each sealed jar with the kind of jelly and the date, and store them in a cool, dark, dry place. If you like, the bands may be removed before the jars are stored.

□ To use paraffin: Paraffin will explode and burn when heated incorrectly. For safety's sake, heat the paraffin in a double boiler until it is hot, but not smoking. Fill the jars ½ inch from the rim and cover them immediately with a layer of hot paraffin ⅛ inch thick. The paraffin must touch all sides of the glass for a proper seal.

Prick any air bubbles that appear in the paraffin.
☐ A single thin layer of paraffin is a better seal than a thick layer.

Mint Jelly

Quantity: Four ½-pint jars of jelly

Ingredients
    4 cups strained hot (tart) apple
        juice
    4 cups white sugar
        water
    ½ cup mint leaves
        green food coloring

Procedure
1. Wash and dry the mint leaves. Pack them firmly into a measuring cup to measure them correctly. Put the measured leaves into a small bowl and pour ½ cup boiling water over them. Let the mint leaves stand for 1 hour. Remove the leaves from the bowl, squeezing as much liquid as possible from them.
2. Follow the directions for Jelly through Step 10. Combine the extracted liquid and the apple juice and continue following the directions for Jelly from Step 11.
3. Add a few drops of green food coloring to the jelly before pouring it into the jars.

Jam

Quantity: Four ½-pint jars of jam

Ingredients
4 cups hot fruit pulp
4 cups white sugar (use 1 cup
    less sugar for sweet fruits
    + 1 tablespoon lemon
    juice)
water

Suggested fruits
raspberries, strawberries, blueberries, gooseberries, plums,
peaches, apricots, figs

Special utensil
pestle or similar object

Procedure
1. Follow the directions for Jelly through Step 9.
2. Pour the cooked fruit into the mixing bowl. If the fruit had a skin, use a pestle or similarly shaped object to force the fruit through a colander into the bowl. The fruit pulp will pass through the holes of the colander and the skins will remain inside. Discard the skins.
3. Follow the directions for Jelly from Step 11 to the finish.

Quince and Rose Geranium Jelly

Quantity: Four ½-pint jars of jelly

Ingredients
4 cups strained hot quince
    juice
4 cups white sugar
    water
8 rose geranium leaves

Procedure

Follow the directions for Jelly. Wash the rose geranium leaves and crush them slightly between your fingers. Place 2 leaves in the bottom of each jar before pouring the hot jelly in the jar.

Egg Specialties

At a glance the recipes in this section would seem to have no direct relationship to each other. The thread that ties them together is the unique properties of the versatile egg. In previous chapters the egg has acted, for example, as a binding agent in cookies, a leavening agent in air foam cakes, and as a flavoring in breads. In this group of recipes, the egg is either the primary or the most significant ingredient.

The egg adds flavor, substance, and leavening to popovers, cream puffs, soufflés, and meringues. It flavors and thickens baked and stirred custards. And hollandaise sauce, béarnaise sauce, and mayonnaise are emulsions made from a fat held in suspension by egg yolks.

Custards

A custard is a mixture of eggs, milk, and various mild flavorings which is heated until the protein in the egg coagulates or thickens the mixture. Custards may be a simple, nourishing dessert when sweetened with sugar, a delicious frozen treat, or a pleasing main dish when cooked with cheese, meats, or vegetables. If the custard is cooked on top of the stove, it is called a stirred custard. Stirred custards are slightly fluid, smooth, and creamy, with a consistency similar to heavy cream. Frozen custard is made from a stirred custard and heavy cream. If the same stirred custard mixture is cooked in the oven, it becomes a baked custard. It has a tender, firm consistency similar to a creamy gelatin-thickened substance. A baked custard may be cut with a knife.

The only trick to making either custard successfully is to avoid overcoagulation of the egg protein. This causes a separation of liquid from the mixture. This separation is called curdling in stirred custards and weeping in baked custards. Overcoagulation is avoided by cooking the mixture at relatively low oven and stove-top temperatures and by taking great care not to overcook the custard. Custards should be watched very carefully as they approach the end of the cooking time, because the egg protein very quickly passes from the point of maximum thickening to curdling or weeping.

Custards must always be stored under refrigeration because they are very susceptible to dangerous bacterial spoilage. This spoilage is usually not apparent.

Dessert Baked Custard

Quantity: *Three cups custard*
Oven Temperature: *325° F.*
Baking Time: *40 minutes*

Ingredients

¼ teaspoon salt
½ cup white sugar
3 extra large eggs
1 cup milk
1 cup half-and-half
1 teaspoon vanilla
¼ teaspoon nutmeg

Utensils

glass measuring cup
set of graduated metal measuring
  cups
set of measuring spoons
medium mixing bowl
colander
fine cheesecloth
wire whisk
wooden spoon
2-quart baking dish
9 x 13 inch cake pan
kitchen timer
2 cooling racks
hot pad

Procedure

1. Read the chapter introduction.
2. Plan to have all the ingredients
at room temperature at the time
you are ready to begin. This
means the eggs and milk should
be removed from the refrigerator
1 hour before mixing the custard.
Measure the milk in the glass
measuring cup and return the rest
to the refrigerator. Don't allow
your entire milk supply to stand at
room temperature as this will
hasten spoilage of the milk.
3. Set out all the ingredients and
utensils in a convenient working
space.

Mixing and baking

1. Preheat the oven to 325°.
2. Break the eggs into a mixing
bowl and beat them with the wire
whisk until they are a uniform
color. Wet the cheesecloth. Wring
out all of the excess water and
line the colander with one or two
thicknesses of the cloth. Place the
colander inside of the second
mixing bowl. Pour the beaten
eggs into the colander. Gather up
all the edges of the cheesecloth
and gently squeeze to force the
eggs through
  This process will remove the
egg chalazae (the whitish spiral
membranes that hold the yolk in
place), which would otherwise be
visible in the finished product.
3. Measure and beat in the milk,
half-and-half, sugar, salt, nutmeg,
and vanilla.
□ Scalding the milk and half-and-
half will reduce the baking time.
□ If you use raw milk, add 10
minutes to the baking time.
4. Pour the custard into the ungreased baking dish. Place the
dish on a cooling rack inside of
the cake pan. Fill the pan with 1
inch of hot, not boiling, water.
Sprinkle a little extra nutmeg on
top of the custard and place it in
the center of the oven, on the
bottom rack. Set your timer for 40
minutes.
□ Baking times may vary depending upon the size of the container
used for baking.
□ The pan of water allows the
custard to cook at a more uniform
rate. The water must never simmer or boil because this will
cause the custard to have a
grainy texture.

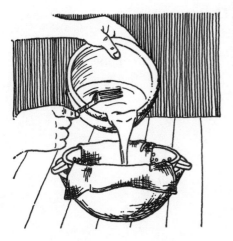

5. When the timer goes off, test the custard for doneness by inserting a knife halfway between the center and edge of the baking dish. When the knife comes out clean, remove the pan from the oven. Take the dish out of the pan of water and place it on a second cooling rack. Test the center of the custard for doneness immediately. It should be slightly underdone. The cooking process is completed as the cus-

tard cools. If the center tests done (the knife comes out clean), cool the custard in a pan of ice water. The cold water will minimize further cooking of the custard.

□ Overcooked custard is objectionable because it weeps. This means that watery liquid separates from the custard.

6. Cool the custard to room temperature. You may serve it at once or chill.

Maple Baked Custard

Quantity: *Three cups custard*
Oven Temperature: *325° F.*
Baking Time: *50 minutes*

Ingredients
¼ teaspoon salt
3 tablespoons white sugar
½ cup real maple syrup
3 extra large eggs
1 extra large egg yolk
¾ cup whole milk
1 cup half-and-half

Procedure
Follow the directions for Dessert Baked Custard.

Caramel Glazed Baked Custard

Quantity: *Three cups custard*
Oven Temperature: *325° F.*
Baking Time: *1 hour*

Ingredients

Custard
¼ teaspoon salt
½ cup white sugar
3 extra large eggs
3 extra large egg yolks
1 cup whole milk
1 cup half-and-half
1 teaspoon vanilla

Caramel
½ cup sugar
1 tablespoon water
¼ cup boiling water

Extra
whipped cream garnish for the
top of the custard

Special utensil
charlotte mold or heavy (nonferrous) pan

Procedure

Preparation
1. Read the chapter introduction.
2. The difficulties of caramelizing sugar and unmolding the baked custard make it absolutely imperative that you use a proper baking dish. A metal charlotte mold works well. These are available in most stores that carry French cooking utensils. (Charlotte molds are not expensive and they make an attractive addition to any kitchen.)
3. Plan to have all the ingredients at room temperature at the time you are ready to begin. This means the eggs and milk should be removed from the refrigerator 1 hour before mixing the custard. Measure out the milk in the glass measuring cup and return the rest to the refrigerator. Don't allow your entire milk supply to stand at room temperature as this will hasten spoilage of the milk. Sepa-

rate 3 of the eggs into the 2 bowls. Set the egg yolks aside and refrigerate or freeze the extra whites for future use.

4. Set out all the ingredients and utensils in a convenient working space.

Mixing and baking

1. Mix and bake the custard following the directions for Dessert Baked Custard. Remember to add the 3 extra egg yolks to the whole eggs. Set the custard mixture aside.

2. Measure the sugar to be caramelized and put it in the charlotte mold (or any nonferrous pan). Add 1 tablespoon of water and stir it in.

3. Put a kettle of water on the stove to boil. You will need the ¼ cup of boiling water to mix with the sugar in 10 minutes.

4. Fill a pan large enough to comfortably hold the charlotte mold with cold water and set it aside.

5. Put the charlotte mold on the stove and turn the heat on to medium. The caramelization process will take about 10 minutes. You will need to watch over and stir the sugar for the entire time. You

cannot leave it unattended for even a few seconds. You will see the sugar in the pan first become very fluid and bubbly. Then it will dry out into small white opaque lumps. Continue stirring this hard sugar, for very shortly it will melt and begin to turn a light brown color. Remove the pan from the heat and add ¼ cup of boiling water very slowly and with a great deal of care. The difference in temperature between the sugar and the water may cause dangerous splattering. Stir in the water and return the pan to the stove. Cook the sugar and water, stirring constantly until the mixture is a beautiful caramel color. Using the small heart-shaped handles and two hot pads, lift the dish off the stove and set it in the pan of cold water until the caramel firms up slightly. Now tilt the mold in all directions to evenly distribute the caramel. When the caramel is no longer runny, invert the mold over a plate to cool.

□ If you did not caramelize the sugar directly in the charlotte mold and must transfer the caramel to a glass or porcelain baking dish, you must first warm up the baking dish. To do this, set the dish in a pan of very hot water for several minutes until the dish becomes hot. Pour the liquid caramel into the dish and tilt the dish in all directions to evenly distribute the caramel. The caramel will not coat the glass or porcelain surface as easily as it coats metal. Allow the caramel to firm up and invert the dish on a plate until you are ready to fill it with the custard.

6. When the charlotte mold has cooled enough to be only lukewarm to the touch, pour the custard into it. Place the pan on a

cooling rack inside of a deep pan.
Fill the pan with enough hot, not
boiling, water to cover the bottom
half of the mold. Place it in the
oven on the lower rack. Set your
timer for 1 hour.

7. Allow the custard to cool to
lukewarm. This should take about
15 to 20 minutes. In the meantime
heat a kettle of water to boiling.

8. Run a knife all around the
edge of the custard to loosen it
from the mold. Pour boiling water
over a towel in the sink. As soon
as the towel cools enough to allow you to touch it, wring out all
the excess water. Set the towel
down, and working very quickly,
place an attractive serving plate
face down on the mold. Set the
mold and plate down on the
steaming towel for a minute. The
heat will loosen the caramel. Now
invert the plate and mold with a
quick motion of the arm. The custard should come out of the mold
and onto the plate. To remove the
caramel remaining in the mold,
add 1 or 2 tablespoons of boiling
water to the pan, stir to loosen
the caramel, and pour the caramel over the unmolded custard.

9. Serve the custard warm or
cold. Garnish the top with Sweet
Whipped Cream, page 183, if you
like.

Main Dish Custard Pie

Quantity: One 9-inch pie
Oven Temperature: 350° F.
Baking Time: 1 hour
Crust preparation time: 1½ hours minimum

Ingredients
½ teaspoon salt
4 extra large eggs
1 tablespoon butter
1 cup whole milk
1 cup half-and-half
grating of pepper
⅛ teaspoon cayenne for the Cheddar cheese pie
⅛ teaspoon nutmeg for the Swiss Cheese pie
¾ cup grated cheese, Cheddar or Swiss
1 small onion
1 9-inch pastry crust

Extra
Optional flavorings: use only one
½ cup diced ham
shredded chicken
3 tablespoons crumbled bacon

Special utensil
pastry brush

Procedure

Preparation
1. Prepare the Pâte Brisée pastry crust, page 105. Line a 9-inch round cake pan with the pastry crust. Refrigerate the crust while preparing the filling.
2. Read the directions for Dessert Baked Custard.

Mixing and baking
1. Preheat the oven to 350°.
2. Measure out the milk and half-and-half in a glass measuring cup and scald it over a low flame. Set the milk aside.
3. Grate and measure the cheese. Prepare the optional meat flavoring if you plan to use it. Set these ingredients aside.
4. Peel and finely chop the onion using a very sharp French knife and the illustrated chopping motion.
□ Chop against a wooden board. Harder surfaces will dull your knife.
5. Melt the butter in the frying pan. Add the chopped onion and sauté over a medium flame until the onion becomes transparent, but not brown. Remove the pan from the stove and set it aside.
□ Stir and watch over the onion the entire time it is cooking. It will burn very quickly.
6. Break 3 eggs into the mixing bowl, and add one extra egg yolk, and beat the eggs with a wire whisk until they are a uniform color. Reserve the egg white for Step 7. Measure and add the salt, pepper, and flavoring to the beaten eggs. Gradually beat in the scalded milk and half-and-half. Continue beating the mixture until it has a uniform color.
7. Remove the pastry crust from the refrigerator. Add 1 teaspoon of water to the reserved egg white. Beat it for a few seconds with a fork. Use a pastry brush to

coat all of the exposed surfaces of the pastry crust lightly with the egg white. Don't glob the egg white on the crust. Spread it thinly and evenly.

8. Transfer the sautéed onions to the pastry crust and spread them evenly around the bottom. Sprinkle the meat flavoring and grated cheese over the onion layer.

9. Pour the custard mixture into the crust and place the pie in the center of the oven on the middle rack. Set your timer.

10. Allow the pie to cool 15 minutes before serving.

Lemon Meringue Custard

Quantity: *Four cups custard*
Oven Temperature: *350° F.*
Baking Time: *50 minutes*

Ingredients

- ½ cup all-purpose flour
- ¼ teaspoon salt
- 1¼ cups superfine white sugar
- 4 extra large eggs
- 2 tablespoons butter
- 1½ cups whole milk
- 2 large lemons
- 1 tablespoon grated lemon rind

Extra

whipped cream for garnish (optional)
fresh berries for garnish (optional)

Procedure

Preparation

1. Read the directions for Dessert Baked Custard. Preheat the oven to 350°.
2. Grate 1 tablespoon of lemon peel. Cut the lemons in half; squeeze them and remove all seeds. Set the lemon juice aside.

Mixing and baking

1. Melt the butter in a small saucepan over a low flame and set it aside to cool slightly.
2. Tear off two pieces of waxed paper approximately 12 inches long. With a metal measuring cup roughly measure out the flour and sift it onto one of the pieces of waxed paper. Move the sifter to the second sheet of waxed paper and measure the flour, salt, and 1 cup of the sugar into the sifter. Pour the excess flour back into its storage container. Run the dry ingredients through the sifter twice, using the waxed paper to catch and transfer them.

3. Transfer the egg yolks to a medium mixing bowl and beat them with the wire whisk until they are a uniform color. Combine the lemon juice and grated lemon peel with the melted butter in the small saucepan. Sift about ⅓ of the dry ingredients over the egg yolks and beat them in with the wire whisk. Beat in ½ of the lemon-butter mixture. Sift another ⅓ of the dry ingredients into the bowl and beat them in. Add the remaining lemon-butter mixture and beat it in. Sift the last ⅓ of the dry ingredients into the bowl and beat them in. Measure the milk in a glass measuring cup. Beat it into the butter.
4. Pour the egg whites into a deep grease-free, straight-sided bowl that is not made from plastic. Measure out the remaining ¼ cup of sugar and set it next to the electric mixer with the measuring spoons.
5. Begin beating the egg whites with the electric mixer set on medium speed. In a short time, large air bubbles will form on the top of the egg whites, while some liquid remains in the bottom of the bowl. The egg whites should still be fluid and transparent. Turn the mixer up to high and gradually add the sugar, tablespoon by tablespoon.
6. Watch the egg whites carefully. Stop the mixer every minute and check to see if the egg whites have reached the stiff peak stage. At the stiff peak stage, the egg white that follows the beaters out of the mixture will hold its shape and form stiff peaks above the rest of the foam. The beaten egg whites will have a glistening

creamy white color. This is when to stop beating them immediately, because at this point the whites contain all of the air they can hold.

□ Overbeaten egg whites are dull and dry, and they break apart when you attempt to mix them with other ingredients. If you overbeat the egg whites you will have to discard them and begin again.

7. Add about ⅓ of the batter to the stiffly beaten egg whites. Using the wire whisk, gently fold the batter into the egg whites. Folding is accomplished by cutting through the egg whites, lifting up a portion and turning it over. Repeat this motion four or five times, turning the bowl slightly each time. Pour remaining batter into bowl; continue folding until batter is a uniform color.

□ The whites will rapidly lose their volume if they are allowed to stand after they are beaten.

8. Pour the custard into the ungreased baking dish. Place the dish on a cooling rack inside of the cake pan. Fill the pan with 1 inch of hot, not boiling, water. Place it in the center of the oven on the bottom rack. Set your timer for 50 minutes.

□ If the custard is overcooked, the meringue will be dry.

9. Serve the custard warm or cold, whichever is your preference. It is delicious served alone or garnished with whipped cream and fresh berries when in season.

Pecan Custard Pie

Quantity: Filling for one 9-inch pie
shell
Oven Temperature: 350° F.
Baking Time: 40 to 50 minutes
Crust preparation time: 1½ hours
minimum

Ingredients

1 tablespoon all-purpose flour
½ teaspoon salt
1 cup brown sugar
½ cup white sugar
2 extra large eggs
½ cup butter
2 tablespoons milk
1 cup pecans (unsalted)
1 9-inch pastry crust

Procedure

Preparation

1. Prepare the Plain Pastry crust,
page 98. Line a 9-inch-diameter
glass pie pan with the pastry crust
and partially bake the crust as described in Rolling Step 17. The
crust should be baked until it is
very light golden brown. Set the
crust aside.
2. Read the directions for Dessert
Baked Custard.

Mixing and baking

1. Preheat the oven to 350°.
2. Melt the butter in a small
saucepan. Measure the milk and
stir it into the butter. Set the butter-milk mixture aside to cool
slightly.
3. Measure the flour, salt, and
sugars into a bowl and mix them
together.
□ For this small quantity of flour it
is not necessary to sift the flour
before measuring it.
4. Break the eggs into the mixing
bowl and beat them with the wire
whisk until they are a uniform
color. Sift ½ of the dry ingredients over the beaten eggs. Beat
them in with the wire whisk. Add
the cooled butter-milk mixture and
beat it in. Sift the remaining dry
ingredients in the bowl and beat
them in.
5. Pour the custard mixture into
the partially baked pastry shell.
Measure out the pecans and
sprinkle them evenly around the
custard filled pastry shell.
□ Whole pecans make a more attractive pie, but broken pecans
will taste the same.
6. Place the pan in the center of
the oven on the middle rack. Set
your timer for 40 minutes.
7. Serve when the Pecan Custard
Pie cools to room temperature.
Store the pie in the refrigerator.

Honey Pumpkin Pie

Quantity: Filling for one 9-inch pie shell
Oven Temperature: 375° F.
Baking Time: 50 minutes
Crust preparation time: 1½ hours minimum

Ingredients

- ½ teaspoon salt
- ¾ cup honey
- 3 extra large eggs
- 1 cup milk
- ½ cup light cream
- 1½ teaspoons cinnamon
- 1 teaspoon ginger
- ¾ teaspoon nutmeg
- 1½ cups of canned cooked pumpkin
- 1 9-inch pastry crust

Extra

Cut a pumpkin out of the extra pastry dough. Bake as directed in Plain Pastry recipe, page 98, Rolling Step 16, and use it to decorate your pumpkin pie.
whipped cream for garnish

Procedure

Preparation

1. Prepare a Plain Pastry, Sweet Pastry, or Cream Cheese Pastry crust. Line a 9-inch-diameter glass pie pan with the crust and partially bake it as described on page 103. The baked crust should be light golden brown. Set the crust aside.
2. Read the directions for Dessert Baked Custard.

Mixing and baking

1. Preheat the oven to 350°.
2. Break the eggs into a small mixing bowl. Beat them with the wire whisk until they are a uniform color. Beat in the milk and cream.
3. Measure out the canned pumpkin and put it in the medium mixing bowl. Measure the honey and beat it into the pumpkin with the wire whisk. Measure and beat in the salt and spices.
□ Dip the measuring cup in boiling water just before measuring the honey.
4. Gradually add the egg-milk mixture to the pumpkin while beating with the wire whisk. Beat the custard until smooth and uniform in color.
5. Pour the custard into the partially baked pastry shell. Place the filled pie pan on a cooling rack inside of the cake pan. Fill the pan with 1 inch of hot, not boiling, water. Place the pan in the center of the oven on the middle rack. Set your timer for 50 minutes.
6. Cool to room temperature before serving. Store the pie in the refrigerator.

Viola McDonald's Rhubarb Custard Pie

Quantity: Filling for one 9-inch
  pie shell
Oven Temperature: 350° F.
Baking Time: 50 minutes
Crust preparation time: 1½ hours
  minimum

Ingredients
2 tablespoons all-purpose flour
1 cup white sugar
2 extra large eggs
2 cups fresh rhubarb
1 tablespoon concentrated orange juice
½ teaspoon grated orange rind
1 9-inch pastry crust

Procedure

Preparation
1. Prepare a Sweet Pastry or
Cream Cheese Pastry crust. Line
a 9-inch-diameter glass pie pan
with the pastry crust and partially
bake the crust as described on
page 000. The baked crust should
be light golden brown. Set the
crust aside.
2. Read the directions for Dessert
Baked Custard.
3. Thaw the frozen orange juice
concentrate enough to allow you
to remove 1 tablespoon. Grate
the orange rind.

4. Set out all the ingredients and
utensils in a convenient working
space.

Mixing and baking
1. Preheat the oven to 350°.
2. Clean the rhubarb and dice it
into ¼-inch-square pieces. Measure out 2 cups of diced rhubarb.
3. Break the eggs into a medium
mixing bowl. Beat them with a
wire whisk until they are a uniform color.
4. Measure out the sugar and
flour into the small mixing bowl.
Stir them with a spoon until they
are well mixed.
5. Gradually add the sugar-flour
mixture to the eggs while beating
with the wire whisk. Beat until the
mixture is smooth.
6. Beat in the orange juice and
orange rind. Stir in the diced rhubarb.
7. Pour the custard into the partially baked pie shell. Place the
pan in the center of the oven on
the middle rack. Set your timer for
50 minutes.
8. Cool to room temperature
before serving. Store the pie in
the refrigerator.

Vanilla Stirred Custard

Quantity: Three cups custard

Ingredients

  6 tablespoons all-purpose flour
  ⅛ teaspoon salt
  ½ cup white sugar
  3 extra large egg yolks
  1 tablespoon soft butter
  2 cups whole milk
  1 teaspoon vanilla

Utensils

glass measuring cup
set of graduated metal measuring
  cups
set of measuring spoons
2 medium mixing bowls
2 small bowls
colander
flour sifter
double boiler
fine cheesecloth
wire whisk
rubber scraper
wooden spoon
waxed paper
kitchen timer
hot pad

Procedure

Preparation

1. Read the chapter introduction.
2. Plan to have the egg yolks and
butter at room temperature when
you are ready to begin. This will
take approximately 1 hour from
the time they are removed from
the refrigerator. Separate the
eggs while they are still cold. For
this, you will need 2 small bowls.
Crack the first egg and split it in
half over 1 of the bowls. Some of
the white will drop out immediately. Hold the yolk in half of the
shell, and by transferring it back
and forth from shell to shell, drain
out the rest of the white. Drop the

yolk into the second empty bowl.
Repeat the process with the second and third eggs. Store the
whites in the refrigerator or
freezer for future use.
3. Set out all the utensils in a
convenient working space.

Mixing and cooking

1. Beat the egg yolks with a wire
whisk until they are a uniform
color. Wet the cheesecloth. Wring
out all of the excess water and
line the colander with one or two
thicknesses of the cloth. Place the
colander inside of a medium mixing bowl. Pour the egg yolks into
the colander. Gather up all the
edges of the cheesecloth and
gently squeeze to force the egg
yolks through. Set the egg yolks
aside.
□ This process will remove the
egg chalazae (whitish spiral membranes that hold the yolk in
place), which would otherwise be
visible in the finished product.

2. Measure out the milk and place
it in the top half of the double
boiler. Fill the lower half of the
double boiler with hot water and

place the entire pan on the stove over a medium heat.

3. While the milk is heating to the scalding point, measure the flour, sugar, and salt. Sift them into a small mixing bowl. Add 2 or 3 tablespoons of the hot milk and stir it in. Add 4 more tablespoons of the milk and stir to make a smooth paste.

4. When the milk is scalded, add the flour-sugar paste and stir until there are no lumps.

5. Cook over the double boiler, stirring slowly and constantly until the mixture is very thick. This should take about 10 minutes. You may wish to set your timer.

□ Rapid stirring cools the mixture.

6. Remove the top pan of the double boiler from the heat and stir the mixture for 1 or 2 minutes to cool it slightly.

7. Add 2 tablespoons of the thickened milk mixture to the egg yolks and stir. Add 2 more tablespoons and stir. Do this a third time, and the egg yolks will have warmed up sufficiently to allow their addition to the hot milk mixture.

□ Eggs added directly to a larger quantity of hot liquid will partially cook on contact with the hot liquid. This will cause lumps of cooked egg in the finished product.

8. Stir the warmed egg yolks into the thickened milk mixture while the pan is still off the stove.

9. Return the pan to the double boiler and reduce the heat slightly. Cook the custard for about 5 minutes, stirring slowly and constantly, or until the custard evenly coats a silver spoon.

□ Eggs must be cooked slowly over low temperatures or they will curdle and cause an unpleasant texture in your custard.

10. Remove the pan from the heat and stir in the softened butter.

11. Cool the custard for 5 minutes in a pan of cold water and stir in the vanilla.

12. Cover the custard with waxed paper while it cools to prevent the formation of a skin on the top. Store the custard in the refrigerator.

Chocolate Stirred Custard

Quantity: Three cups custard

Ingredients

½ cup all-purpose flour
⅛ teaspoon salt
⅔ cup white sugar
3 extra large egg yolks
1 tablespoon soft butter
2 cups milk
2 1-ounce squares un-
    sweetened chocolate
1 teaspoon vanilla

Procedure

Follow the directions for Vanilla Stirred Custard. Cut the chocolate squares into quarters and dissolve them in the scalded milk.

Banana Custard Pie

*Quantity: Filling for one 9-inch
pie shell*
*Crust preparation time: 1½ hours
minimum*

Ingredients

6 tablespoons all-purpose flour
⅛ teaspoon salt
½ cup white sugar
3 extra large egg yolks
1 tablespoon butter
2 cups milk
1 teaspoon vanilla
2 medium-size ripe bananas
1 lime (optional)
1 9-inch pastry crust

Extra

whipped cream for the top of the
    pie
one sliced banana for garnish

Procedure

1. Prepare a Plain Pastry, Sweet Pastry, or Cream Cheese Pastry crust. Line a 9-inch-diameter glass pie pan with the pastry crust and thoroughly bake it as described on pages 103–104. Cool the baked crust to room temperature.
2. While the pastry crust is cooling, prepare the custard filling following the directions for Vanilla Stirred Custard. Cool the custard to room temperature.
□ Remember to place a piece of waxed paper directly on top of the custard while it cools.
3. Peel and slice 2 of the bananas. Squeeze the lime and pour 1 tablespoon of juice over the bananas. Lightly toss them to evenly distribute the juice. Set the rest of the juice aside.

□ The lime juice will retard the discoloration of the bananas.

4. Line the bottom of the cooled pie crust with an even layer of sliced banana. Pour the cooled custard over the bananas. Refrigerate the pie until a few minutes before serving time. Prepare Sweetened Whipped Cream, page 183. Cover the top of the pie with the whipped cream, making decorative swirls with a knife or spatula. Slice the last banana. Toss it with 1 tablespoon of lime juice and arrange the slices around the top of the pie. Serve at once. Store the pie in the refrigerator.

Lemon Custard Pie

Quantity: Filling for one 9-inch pie shell

Crust preparation time: 1½ hours minimum

Ingredients

  5 tablespoons all-purpose flour
  ¼ teaspoon salt
  ¾ cup white sugar
  3 extra-large egg yolks
1½ tablespoons butter
  1 cup boiling water
  ¼ cup lemon juice
  1 tablespoon grated lemon rind
  1 9-inch pastry crust

Extra

soft meringue for the top of the pie, page 185

Procedure

Preparation

1. Prepare a Plain Pastry or Sweet Pastry crust. Line a 9-inch-diameter glass pie pan with the pastry crust and thoroughly bake it as directed on pages 103–104. Cool the baked crust to room temperature.
2. Read the directions for Vanilla Stirred Custard.
3. Grate the lemon peel. Squeeze and measure the lemon juice. Remove all seeds from the juice.

Mixing and cooking

1. Beat the egg yolks with a wire whisk until they are a uniform color. Wet the cheesecloth. Wring out all of the excess water and line the colander with one or two thicknesses of the cloth. Place the colander inside of a medium mixing bowl. Pour the egg yolks into the colander. Gather up all the edges of the cheesecloth and gently squeeze to force the egg yolks through. Set the egg yolks aside.

□ This process will remove the egg chalazae (whitish spiral membranes that hold the yolk in place), which would otherwise be visible in the finished product.

2. Put a kettle of water on the stove to boil. You will need 1 cup of boiling water. Fill the lower half of the double boiler with hot water and place it on the stove over a medium heat.
3. Measure out the flour, salt, and sugar into a medium mixing bowl. Stir to combine them.
4. When the water reaches boiling, measure it out in a glass measuring cup. Add the boiling water 4 tablespoons at a time to the sifted dry ingredients, stirring in each water addition with the wire whisk.
5. Transfer the mixture to the top half of the double boiler and cook directly over the flame, stirring slowly and constantly until the mixture is very thick. This should take about 5 minutes. You may wish to set your timer.
6. Remove the pan from the heat and stir mixture for 1 or 2 minutes to cool it slightly.
7. Add 2 tablespoons of the thickened mixture to the egg yolks and stir. Add 2 more tablespoons and stir. Do this a third time, and the egg yolks will have warmed up sufficiently to allow their addition to the hot, thickened mixture.

□ Egg added directly to a larger quantity of hot liquid will partially cook on contact with the hot liquid. This will cause lumps of cooked egg in the finished custard.

8. Stir the warmed egg yolks into the thickened mixture while the pan is still off the stove.

9. Place the pan over the bottom of the double boiler. Cook the mixture for about 5 minutes, stirring slowly and constantly, until the mixture just begins to boil.

□ Eggs must be cooked slowly over low temperatures or they will curdle and cause an unpleasant texture.

10. Remove from the heat and stir in the softened butter.

11. Cool the mixture for 5 minutes by placing top of double boiler in a pan of cold water, and stir in the lemon juice and grated rind.

12. Cool the lemon custard to room temperature. Cover the top with waxed paper while it cools to prevent the formation of a skin on the top.

13. Pour the cooled lemon pudding into the baked pastry crust. Prepare and bake a soft meringue, using the reserved egg whites, page 185. Store the pie in the refrigerator.

Chocolate Custard Pie

Quantity: Filling for one 9-inch pie shell
Crust preparation time: 1½ hours minimum

Ingredients
6 tablespoons all-purpose flour
⅛ teaspoon salt
⅔ cup white sugar
3 extra large egg yolks
1 tablespoon soft butter
2 cups milk
2 1-ounce squares un-
    sweetened chocolate
½ cup chocolate chips
¼ cup chopped almonds
1 teaspoon vanilla
1 9-inch pastry crust

Extra
1 pint heavy cream, whipped
    for the top of the pie
¼ cup chopped or slivered al-
    monds (with skins) to gar-
    nish whipped cream

Procedure
1. Prepare a Cream Cheese Pastry crust. Line a 9-inch-diameter glass pie pan with the pastry crust and thoroughly bake it as described on pages 103–104.

Sprinkle the chocolate chips evenly around the bottom of the pie crust as soon as you remove it from the oven. Return the crust to the oven until the chocolate becomes very soft. This should take only 1 or 2 minutes. Smooth the chocolate out with a knife and sprinkle the chopped almonds evenly around the melted chocolate. Cool the crust to room temperature.

2. While the pastry crust is cooling, prepare the custard filling following the instructions given for Chocolate Stirred Custard. Cool the custard to room temperature.
□ Remember to place a piece of waxed paper directly on top of the custard while it cools.

3. Pour the cooled custard into the pastry shell. Refrigerate the pie until a few minutes before serving time. Prepare Sweetened Whipped Cream, see page 183. Cover the top of the pie with whipped cream, making decorative swirls with a knife or spatula. Sprinkle the almonds reserved for garnish around the whipped cream. Serve at once. Store the pie in the refrigerator.

Vanilla Frozen Custard

Quantity: One-half gallon
Preparation time: 24 hours

Ingredients
4 tablespoons all-purpose flour
½ teaspoon salt
1 cup white sugar
2 extra large egg yolks
2 cups milk
2 cups heavy cream (2-day-old cream gives the best texture)
3 teaspoons vanilla

Extra

Optional flavorings
1 cup roasted salted nuts
1 cup chocolate chips
1 cup broken peppermint candy
1 cup very finely chopped fresh fruit which has been soaked in cognac, rum, or kirsch for 3 hours

Special utensils
ice cream freezer, 1-gallon capacity or larger
10 pounds ice
rock salt
one-half gallon storage container

Procedure

Preparation
1. Follow the directions for Vanilla Stirred Custard. Don't add the vanilla or cream to the custard.
2. Measure out the cream in a glass measuring cup and scald it over a low flame on the stove.
□ Scalding the cream improves the texture and flavor of the frozen custard.
3. Combine the scalded cream and thickened custard, and transfer them to a storage container. Chill the mixture in the refrigerator for 8 hours or overnight.

Freezing
1. Before beginning the freezing process, be sure you have at least 10 pounds of ice cubes or chips and several cups of rock salt on hand.
□ Rock salt is very coarse and has less tendency to cake during the freezing process.
2. Wash the ice cream container to remove any traces of salt or rust from previous use.
3. Remove the custard mixture from the refrigerator and stir in the vanilla. Pour the mixture into the interior container of the ice cream freezer. Assemble the freezer.
□ The container should never be more than ¾ full to allow for expansion of the custard during the freezing process.
4. Fill the bottom of the larger freezer container with 2 inches of ice. Sprinkle a handful of rock salt over the ice. Add another 2-inch layer of ice and handful of rock salt. Continue this layering process until the ice fills the container to the very top.

□ There should be a run-off device to prevent the salty water from running into the interior container.

5. If your freezer is the hand-crank variety, begin cranking very slowly. This will allow the mixture inside to cool uniformly and give the finished product a finer texture. As the mixture continues to freeze, the speed at which you are cranking should be increased. As the mixture begins to freeze, cranking will become extremely difficult and finally nearly impossible. At this point the custard is frozen. It should be allowed to chill (ripen) in the salt-ice-water brine undisturbed for ½ hour. Set your timer.

Continue adding ice and small amounts of rock salt as needed during the cranking and ripening processes. You should maintain the original salt-ice level at all times.

6. When the custard has ripened, remove the interior container from the freezer. Pull the beater out of the container and scrape the custard from the beater or, if you can't resist, lick the custard from the beater. Stir in any of the extra additions to the custard at this time. Drain the liquor from the fresh fruit before adding it to the custard. Transfer the frozen custard to the storage container and place it in the freezer for 4 hours before serving.

□ The liquor will prevent the pieces of fresh fruit from freezing into solid little lumps when the custard is frozen.

7. If your freezer is electric, plug it in after filling it with ice. Keep an eye on the ice level while the custard is freezing and listen carefully for the slowing or stopping of the machine. If the machine is allowed to continue running after it has stopped cranking, the motor will burn out in a very short time. If the freezer does not stop cranking, check the custard mixture after ½ hour (set your timer). The custard will resemble very heavy whipped cream when it has been cranked enough. Begin the ripening process when the custard looks like this.

Chocolate Frozen Custard

Quantity: One-half gallon

Ingredients
4 tablespoons all-purpose flour
½ teaspoon salt
1¼ cups white sugar
2 extra large egg yolks
2 cups milk
2 cups heavy cream (1 pint)
2 teaspoons vanilla
4 1-ounce squares of un-
    sweetened chocolate

Extra
1 cup roasted salted nuts

Special Utensils
ice cream freezer, 1-gallon capac-
    ity or larger
10 pounds ice
rock salt
one-half gallon storage container

Procedure
Follow the directions for Vanilla
Frozen Custard. Cut the chocolate into small pieces and melt
them in the scalded milk.

Popovers and Cream Puffs

Popovers are different from most quick breads because they use no chemical leavening agent. They are made from an egg, flour, butter, and milk batter that is usually baked in a muffin pan at a very high temperature. Steam forms within the batter causing the tops of the popover to push up over the sides of the pan. The tops are distorted by the uneven pressure of the steam, and the end result is a beautiful, light and airy, golden brown structure, which when served with butter and jam makes a delightful breakfast dish.

Popover batter made with beef drippings as well as butter and baked in a dish becomes the familiar Yorkshire pudding.

Cream puffs are made utilizing the same principles as popovers. They differ in a few ways. The batter is made with a higher proportion of butter. Water replaces the milk used in popovers. The resulting pastelike batter is dropped by spoonfuls onto a baking sheet. The baked cream puff shells are traditionally filled with whipped cream or custard and topped with powdered sugar or chocolate sauce.

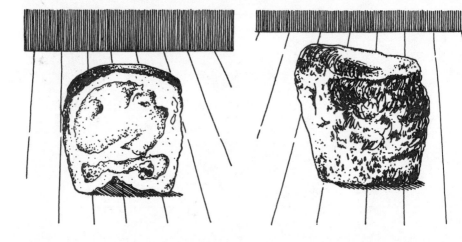

Popovers

Quantity: One dozen popovers
Oven Temperature: 450° F. for 15
   minutes, 350° F. for 20 minutes
Baking Time: 35 minutes

Ingredients
1 cup all-purpose flour
½ teaspoon salt
3 extra large eggs
1 tablespoon butter
1 cup cold milk

Extra
butter for greasing the muffin pan

Utensils
glass measuring cup
set of graduated metal measuring
   cups
set of measuring spoons
medium mixing bowl
flour sifter
small saucepan
wire whisk
muffin pan
waxed paper
kitchen timer
hot pad

Procedure
1. Read the chapter introduction.
2. Set out all the ingredients and utensils in a convenient working space.
3. Turn the oven on to 450°.
4. Tear off two pieces of waxed paper approximately 12 inches long. With a metal measuring cup roughly measure out the flour and sift it onto one of the pieces of waxed paper. Move the sifter to the second sheet of waxed paper,
and measure the flour and salt into the sifter. Run the flour through the sifter one more time. Set the flour aside.
5. Melt the butter in the small saucepan. Set it aside.
6. Grease the muffin pan generously with the extra butter. Place the pan in the oven for 3 minutes while you mix up the batter.
□ The best popovers are made by pouring the freshly mixed batter into a preheated pan.
7. Place the flour in the mixing bowl and stir in the milk in small additions, beating in each addition with the wire whisk.
□ Adding the cold milk in small additions and beating each addition into the flour will prevent the flour from lumping.
8. Beat in the eggs, one at a time.
9. Beat in the melted butter. The batter should be smooth and evenly mixed.
□ Do not continue beating the batter beyond this point.
10. Remove the muffin pan from the oven and distribute the batter evenly among the wells of the tin. Each well should be about ¾ full.
11. Place the filled muffin pan in the oven in the center of the lower rack. Set your timer for 15 minutes. When the timer goes off, reduce the oven heat to 350° and reset the timer for 20 minutes.
□ Do not open the oven door even a crack during the baking time. You will cause the collapse of your popovers.
12. Remove the popovers from the oven and serve at once.

Cream Puffs

Quantity: *12 to 16 large puffs*
Oven Temperature: *450° F. for
  10 minutes, 400° F. for 25
  minutes*
Baking Time: *35 minutes*

Ingredients
  1 cup sifted all-purpose flour
  ¼ teaspoon salt
  4 extra large eggs
  ½ cup butter
  1 cup water

Extra

Filling
Sweetened Whipped Cream
  (page 183) or Vanilla Stirred
  Custard (page 170)

Topping
Chocolate Sauce (page 184) or
  powdered sugar

Special utensil
ungreased baking sheet

Procedure
1. Read the chapter introduction.
2. Set out all the ingredients
and utensils in a convenient working space.
3. Turn the oven on to 450°.
4. Tear off two pieces of waxed
paper approximately 12 inches
long. With a metal measuring cup
roughly measure out the flour and
sift it onto one of the pieces of
waxed paper. Measure the flour
exactly and sift it onto the second
sheet of waxed paper. Set the
flour aside.
5. Measure out the water in a
glass measuring cup and pour it
into the medium-size saucepan.
Bring the water to boil over medium heat.

□ Don't allow the water to boil
away on the stove. The loss of
water due to evaporation will seriously alter the proportions of the
recipe and may cause the butter
to separate from the flour in Step
7. If this happens, carefully add
more water.
6. Add the butter and salt to the
boiling water and stir until the
butter is dissolved.
7. When the water begins to boil
again, gradually beat in the flour
with the wire whisk. Continue
beating the mixture over the heat
until it pulls away from the sides
of the pan. This will take only 1
or 2 minutes.
8. Remove the pan from the heat
and beat in the eggs one at a
time. Continue beating the mixture until it is smooth and glossy.
The batter will be very stiff.
9. Scoop the batter out in heap-
ing tablespoons and arrange it on
the ungreased baking sheet in
even rows leaving 3 inches in all
directions between cream puffs.
10. Place the baking sheet in the
oven in the center of the middle
rack. Set the timer for 10 minutes.
When the timer goes off, reduce
the oven temperature to 400°. Reset the timer for 25 minutes.
11. When the cream puffs are a
beautiful golden brown, remove
them from the oven and cool
them on the cooling rack.
12. For a custard filling: Prepare
the Vanilla Stirred Custard. While
the custard is cooling, prepare
the Chocolate Sauce.
13. Slice each cream puff in half
and fill the bottom with 1 to 2
spoonfuls of custard. Replace the
top and spoon warm chocolate
sauce over the top. Refrigerate

the cream puffs until you are ready to serve them. Try to serve them within 2 or 3 hours.

□ The shell will become soggy if the assembled cream puffs are left in the refrigerator too long.

14. For a whipped cream filling:

Prepare the Sweetened Whipped Cream. Slice each shell in half, fill the bottom with whipped cream and replace the top. Use your flour sifter to sift powdered sugar over the tops of the filled cream puffs. Serve at once.

Sweetened Whipped Cream

Quantity: Two cups whipped cream

Ingredients
1 cup chilled heavy cream (½ pint)
2 tablespoons powdered sugar
1 teaspoon vanilla

Procedure
1. Chill the bowl and beaters as well as the cream.
2. Set the powdered sugar, vanilla, and measuring spoons near the electric mixer.
3. Remove the cream, bowl, and beaters from the refrigerator.
4. Pour the cream into the bowl, assemble the mixer, and begin whipping the cream. Rotate the beaters all around the bowl and gradually increase the speed of the mixer to medium.

5. Beat to the desired consistency, but do not beat the cream until it becomes too stiff and turns to butter. There is no remedy for this.
6. Fold in the sugar and vanilla with the wire whisk.

Tips about whipped cream
1. Whipped cream has approximately twice the volume of unwhipped cream.
2. The whipped cream will retain a better volume when it is folded into cold mixtures.
3. Two-day-old cream gives the best volume.
4. Always fold whipped cream into other mixtures. Never beat or stir it in.
5. Whipped cream may be refrigerated for 3 to 4 hours before serving, though some liquid may drain out of it during this period.

Chocolate Sauce

Quantity: One cup sauce

Ingredients
½ cup white sugar
¼ cup honey
¼ teaspoon salt
2 extra large egg yolks
¼ cup heavy cream
¼ cup butter
3 1-ounce squares of un-
  sweetened chocolate

Procedure
1. Set out all of the ingredients and utensils in a convenient working space.
2. Separate the eggs into the 2 small bowls. Transfer the whites to a storage container and refrigerate them for future use. Set the yolks aside.

3. Fill the bottom of the double boiler with water and heat it to a slow boil.
4. Measure out all of the ingredients except the egg yolks and put them in the top of the double boiler. Place the top of the double boiler over the heated water and stir all the ingredients until they are a uniform consistency.
5. Remove the pan from the heat. Beat in the egg yolks one at a time. Return the pan to the heat and continue cooking the mixture, stirring constantly, for 3 minutes.
6. Remove from the heat, cover, and cool for 15 minutes before spooning over the tops of the Cream Puffs, or spoon hot over very frozen ice cream and serve at once.

Meringues

A meringue is a simple egg white foam flavored with sugar. The ratio of sugar to egg whites determines whether the meringue is hard or soft when baked. Soft meringues are usually used to top pies and other dishes. Hard meringues are used as dessert shells and served with a variety of fillings. An unusual combination of hard and soft meringue is baked in a springform pan and served with fruit and whipped cream.

The egg whites in a soft meringue are beaten only to the soft peak stage, and they puff up in the oven during baking. A soft meringue is correctly baked when it puffs up and a pleasing brown color develops on the ridges of the meringue only.

The egg whites in a hard meringue are beaten to the stiff peak stage, and they puff up in the oven during baking. A hard meringue should be snow white and easy to cut without being brittle and breaking apart.

Proper oven temperatures and timings are critical to the success of both meringues. Tough meringues are caused by overbaking, and brown meringues by an oven temperature which is too high.

Soft Meringue

Quantity: Topping for one 9-inch pie
Oven Temperature: 350° F.
Baking Time: 15 to 20 minutes

Ingredients
3 extra large egg whites
6 tablespoons powdered or superfine white sugar
1 teaspoon cream of tartar

Extra
granulated sugar

Utensils
set of measuring spoons
straight-sided mixing bowl
2 small bowls
electric mixer
spatula
kitchen timer
cooling rack
hot pad

Procedure
1. Read the chapter introduction.
2. One hour before the time you have set aside to mix a meringue, remove the eggs from the refrigerator. Separate them while they are cold. For this, you will need 3 small bowls, all of them clean and grease free. Crack the first egg and split it in half over one of the bowls. Some of the white will drop into the bowl immediately. Hold the yolk in half of the shell,

and, by transferring it back and forth from shell to shell, drain out the rest of the white. Drop the yolk into the second empty bowl and with your finger scrape out any white still remaining in the shell. Pour each yolk-free white into the third bowl. Repeat the process for each egg. Set the separated eggs aside until they reach room temperature.

□ Egg whites will achieve a greater volume if beaten when they are at room temperature.

□ Never put egg whites in a plastic bowl.

□ The egg white should be completely free of any traces of the fat-containing egg yolk. Egg whites will not foam properly if they contain fat. Remove any specks of egg yolk from the white with a piece of broken eggshell. If by some misfortune the egg yolk breaks and spills completely into the white, transfer this egg to a storage container and refrigerate it for future use in a whole egg mixture. Wash out the bowl and begin again.

3. Prepare and assemble the pie crust and pie filling. Turn the oven on to 350°.

4. Measure out the sugar and set it next to the electric mixer with the cream of tartar and the measuring spoons.

5. Transfer the egg whites to a deep, straight-sided bowl. The bowl should have no traces of grease left in it from previous use.

6. Begin beating the egg whites with your electric mixer set on medium speed. In a short time, large air bubbles will form on the top of the egg whites while some liquid remains in the bottom of the bowl. The egg whites should still be fluid and transparent. Stop the mixer for a minute, and measure and add the cream of tartar and 2 or 3 tablespoons of the previously measured sugar to the egg whites. Turn the mixer on to high and continue beating while adding the balance of the sugar tablespoon by tablespoon.

□ Be sure the beaters for your electric mixer are completely grease free.

□ Don't dump the sugar in all at once. You must gradually add it to the egg whites.

7. In 1 or 2 minutes stop the mixer and pull out the beaters. The egg whites should have reached the soft peak stage by now. The bubbles should be getting smaller and the foam white. As you remove the beaters, the egg whites that follow the beaters out of the mixture will bend over into soft curls.

8. Immediately spread the meringue over the warm pie filling, sealing it carefully to the crust. Make one or two long swirls around the pie with a spatula. Sprinkle the meringue lightly with granulated sugar.

□ If the meringue is not sealed to the crust, it will shrink away from the crust as it cools.

□ The sugar will make the baked meringue easier to cut.

9. Place the meringue-covered pie in the oven in the center of the middle rack and set your timer for 15 minutes.

10. When the timer goes off, check the meringue. It should have a brown color along the ridges.

□ Do not overbrown the meringue or it will become tough.

11. When you cut the pie, dip the knife in cold water before each cut made through the meringue.

Hard Meringue

Quantity: One dozen 2½-inch
    meringues
Oven Temperature: 225° F.
Baking Time: 70 minutes

Ingredients
    3 extra large egg whites
    ¾ cup powdered or superfine
        white sugar
    1 teaspoon cream of tartar
    1 teaspoon vanilla

Extra
whipped cream and fruit to top
    meringue

Procedure
1. Read the chapter introduction.
2. Cut and cover the baking sheet
with the waxed or brown paper.
3. Turn the oven on to 225°.
4. Follow the directions for a Soft
Meringue through Step 7.
5. Turn the mixer back on to high
and continue beating and watching carefully. The egg whites will
very quickly reach the stiff peak
stage. This is when you stop beating them, immediately, because at
this point the whites contain all of
the air they can hold. When the
beaters are at the stiff peak stage,
the egg whites that follow the
beaters out of the mixture will

hold its shape and form stiff
peaks above the rest of the foam.
The mixture is a glistening creamy
white.
□ Overbeaten egg whites are dull
and dry, and they break apart
when you attempt to mix them
with other ingredients. If you
overbeat the egg whites you will
have to discard them and begin
again.
6. Fold in the vanilla with the
wire whisk.
7. Heap into 12 rounds on the
baking sheet or shape with a
pastry bag and place in the oven
in the center of the middle rack.
Set your timer.
8. When the timer goes off, remove the meringues from the
oven and cool on the cooling
rack. The meringues should be
pure white. They are never allowed to brown.
9. Serve with whipped cream and
fruit. Store leftover meringues in
an airtight container for they
quickly absorb moisture.

Baking variations
□ A 200° oven for 2½ hours will
give a dryer, crunchy meringue.
□ A 275° oven for 1 hour will give
a softer, chewy meringue.

George McDonald's Meringue Cake

Quantity: One 9-inch round cake
Oven Temperature: 500° F.
Baking Time: 2 minutes at 500°,
 8 hours with oven shut off

Ingredients
 10 extra large egg whites
 2½ cups superfine white sugar
 ¼ teaspoon salt
 2½ teaspoons cream of tartar

Extra
2 cups unsweetened whipped
 cream (½ pint cream before
 whipping)
12-ounce can drained sour cherries or 1 to 2 cups fresh
 strawberries
□ Don't sweeten the cream or the
fruit. The cake is very sweet.

Special utensil
springform pan, 9-inch diameter

Procedure
1. Preheat the oven to 500°.
2. Follow the directions for a Soft
Meringue. Add the salt with the
first addition of sugar. You will
have to work very quickly to add
this greater amount of sugar to
the egg whites before they reach
the stiff peak stage.
3. Turn the batter into an ungreased springform pan. Place in
the center of the 500° oven on
the middle rack. Turn the oven
completely off after 1 minute. Do
not open the oven door for 8
hours. Remove the cake from the
pan and refrigerate until you are
ready to serve it.
□ You must have a well-insulated
oven which holds heat for a long
time to be successful with this
cake.
4. Just before serving, heap the
whipped cream on the top of the
cake and decorate it with the fruit.
This cake should be served the
first day after it is baked.

Soufflés

The soufflé is the temperamental queen of all egg dishes. It is made by folding an egg white foam into a thick white sauce and immediately baking the mixture until it poufs up into a light, delicate soufflé. A successful soufflé can add a magnificent touch to a dinner. But before you attempt to serve a soufflé to guests, be sure to practice it at less critical meals until you master the technique.

The following points cannot be stressed often enough in the preparation of a successful soufflé.

1. Beat the egg whites only to the soft peak stage and stabilize the egg foam with cream of tartar or an acid.

2. If a fat film develops on the white sauce, thin it with liquid before folding in the egg whites (see Sauces, page 203). A very thick sauce will not combine successfully with the egg white foam.

3. Mix the soufflé with great speed and bake it immediately.

4. A soufflé should be baked only in an oven which is heated from the bottom.

5. Serve the soufflé the minute it is removed from the oven.

Cheese Soufflé

Quantity: One 8-inch soufflé
Oven Temperature: 350° F.
Baking Time: 35 to 40 minutes

Ingredients

White sauce
3 tablespoons butter
3 tablespoons all-purpose flour
1½ cups cold milk
1 teaspoon salt
⅛ teaspoon pepper
dash cayenne pepper

Egg mixture
¾ cup grated sharp Cheddar cheese
6 extra large eggs
¼ teaspoon cream of tartar

Extra
butter to grease the soufflé dish
grated cheese to dust the greased dish
hollandaise sauce for garnish

Utensils
glass measuring cup
set of metal measuring spoons
medium mixing bowl
3 small bowls
electric mixer
heavy saucepan
wire whisk
hand grater
2-quart soufflé dish (8-inch diameter x 3-inch depth)
9 x 13 inch cake pan
paper or aluminum collar
2 cooling racks
hot pad

Procedure

Preparation

1. Read the chapter introduction.
2. One hour before the time you have set aside to mix a soufflé, remove the eggs from the refrigerator. Separate them while they are cold. For this, you will need 3 small bowls, all of them clean and grease free. Crack the first egg and split it in half over one of the bowls. Some of the white will drop into the bowl immediately. Hold the yolk in half of the shell, and, by transferring it back and forth from shell to shell, drain out the rest of the white. Drop the yolk into the second empty bowl and with your finger scrape out any white still remaining in the shell. Pour each yolk-free white into the third bowl. Repeat the process for each egg. Set the separated eggs aside until they reach room temperature.

☐ Never put egg whites in a plastic bowl.

☐ The egg white should be completely free of any traces of the fat-containing egg yolk. Egg whites will not foam properly if they contain fat. Remove any specks of egg yolk from the white with a piece of broken eggshell. If by some misfortune the egg yolk breaks and spills completely into the white, transfer this egg to a storage container and refrigerate it for future use in a whole egg mixture. Wash out the bowl and begin again.

3. Set out all of the ingredients and utensils in a convenient working space.
4. Grate and measure out the cheese.
5. Grease the sides of the soufflé dish with butter and dust with grated cheese.

☐ Do not grease the sides of the dish without adding the cheese coating. The soufflé will not rise as well on the slippery sides of the dish. The cheese gives the soufflé a textured surface to cling to.

6. Tear off a piece of aluminum foil 30 inches long. Fold it in half lengthwise and in half again. Wrap the aluminum foil collar around the inside of the dish. Pull the ends of the foil tightly together and fold the excess foil together. The collar should stay in place with no additional fastening. It should extend 2 inches above the top rim of the dish.
7. Set the dish and collar on a cooling rack that has been placed inside a cake pan. Fill the cake pan with 1 inch of hot (not boiling) water. Set it aside.

Mixing and baking

1. Preheat the oven to 350°.
2. Prepare a white sauce using the procedure described for making the Thick White Sauce.
3. Remove the pan from the stove. Stir in the seasonings and cheese.
4. Beat the egg yolks until they are a uniform color. Add 2 or 3 tablespoons of white sauce to the egg yolks and blend them in. Make two more small separate additions of white sauce to the egg yolks and blend each addition in.
5. Add the warmed egg yolks to the white sauce. Stir to blend. Set the mixture aside.
6. Pour the egg whites into a deep straight-sided bowl. Set the cream of tartar and the measuring spoons next to the electric mixer.
7. Begin beating egg whites with your electric mixer set at medium speed. In a short time large air bubbles will form on the top of

the egg whites while some liquid remains in the bottom of the bowl. The egg whites should still be fluid and transparent. Stop the mixer for a minute, measure and add the cream of tartar to the egg whites. Turn the mixer on high and continue beating.

8. In 1 or 2 minutes, stop the mixer and pull out the beaters. The egg whites should have reached the soft peak stage by now. As you remove the beaters, the whites that follow the beaters out of the mixture bend over in soft curls. Stop beating the egg whites at this stage.

9. Working very quickly, remove the bowl from the mixer and add about ½ of the egg whites to the sauce. Fold the whites into the sauce. Folding is accomplished by cutting through the whites, lifting up a portion of them, and turning this over. Repeat this motion three or four times, turning the bowl slightly each time.

10. Add the balance of the sauce to the egg white mixture and fold it in until the mixture is a uniform color.

11. Pour the batter into the soufflé dish and make a groove with the rubber scraper 1½ inches

deep all around the top of the soufflé. The groove should be 1¼ inches from the edge of the dish. Immediately place the dish and pan of hot water in the center of the oven on the middle rack. Set your timer for 35 minutes. Do not open the door until the timer goes off.

12. When the timer goes off, check the soufflé for doneness by inserting a knife in the center. If the knife comes out clean, remove the foil collar and serve the soufflé at once. If the knife does not come out clean, return the soufflé to the oven for another 5 minutes.

Vegetable Soufflé

Quantity: One 8-inch soufflé
Oven Temperature: 350° F.
Baking Time: 40 to 50 minutes

Ingredients

White sauce
  3 tablespoons butter
  3 tablespoons all-purpose flour
1½ cups cold milk
  1 teaspoon salt
 ⅛ teaspoon pepper
 ¼ teaspoon onion powder

Egg mixture
  1 cup puréed vegetable, lightly
     salted: corn, spinach,
     broccoli, asparagus
  6 extra large eggs
 ¼ teaspoon cream of tartar
  2 tablespoons freshly grated
     Parmesan cheese

Extra

¼ teaspoon of nutmeg may be
   added to the purée of spinach,
   broccoli, or asparagus
⅛ teaspoon cayenne pepper may
   be added to the purée of corn

butter to grease the soufflé dish
grated cheese to dust the greased
  dish
hollandaise sauce for garnish

Procedure

Use a fresh vegetable, if possible.
Boil the vegetable until tender in a
small amount of water. For spinach, broccoli, and asparagus, this
will take 5 minutes or less. Drain
the vegetable and purée in a
blender. Measure out 1 cup of
vegetable and set it aside. Follow
the directions for the Cheese
Soufflé. Add the puréed vegetable and Parmesan cheese to the
Thick White Sauce at Mixing and
Baking Step 3. Grease the sides
of the soufflé dish lightly with
butter and coat them with freshly
grated Parmesan cheese.
□ Do not grease the sides of the
dish without adding the cheese
coating. The soufflé will not rise
as well on the slippery sides of
the dish. The cheese gives the
soufflé a textured surface to
cling to.

Rosa Hamilton's Chocolate Soufflé

Quantity: One 8-inch soufflé
Oven Temperature: 400° F. for 15
  minutes, 375° F. for 25 minutes
Baking Time: 40 to 50 minutes

Ingredients

White sauce
  3 tablespoons butter
  3 tablespoons all-purpose flour
  1 cup whole milk
  ⅛ teaspoon salt
  ½ cup superfine white sugar

Other ingredients
2½ 1-ounce squares un-
      sweetened chocolate
  5 extra large eggs
  1 extra large egg white
  1 teaspoon cream of tartar
  1 teaspoon vanilla

Extra

butter to grease the soufflé dish
sugar to dust the greased dish
powdered sugar to dust the top of
    the soufflé
whipped cream for garnish

Procedure

1. Preheat the oven to 400°.
2. Follow the directions for the
Cheese Soufflé. Cut the chocolate into small pieces and melt it
in the Thick White Sauce.
3. You may grease the sides of
the soufflé dish lightly with butter
and coat them with granulated
white sugar if you like a chewy
crust.
□ Do not grease the sides of the
dish without adding the sugar
coating. The soufflé will not rise
as well on the slippery sides of
the dish. The sugar gives the
soufflé a textured surface to
cling to.
4. Bake the soufflé at 400° for
15 minutes. Turn the heat down
to 375° and bake it for an additional 25 minutes.

Lemon Soufflé

Quantity: *One 8-inch soufflé*
Oven Temperature: *400° F. for 15 minutes, 375° F. for 25 minutes*
Baking Time: *25 to 30 minutes*

Ingredients

White sauce
  3 tablespoons butter
  3 tablespoons all-purpose flour
  ¾ cup water
  ⅛ teaspoon salt
  ½ cup superfine white sugar

Other ingredients
  4 extra large eggs
  1 extra large egg white
  3 tablespoons lemon juice
    grated rind of a lemon
  ½ teaspoon vanilla

Extra

butter to grease the soufflé dish
granulated sugar to dust the
  greased dish
powdered sugar to dust the top of
  the soufflé
whipped cream for garnish

Preparation

1. Grate the lemon rind. Squeeze and measure the lemon juice.
2. Preheat the oven to 400°.
3. Prepare the soufflé following the directions for the Cheese Soufflé. Add the grated lemon rind and vanilla to the white sauce. The lemon juice replaces the cream of tartar and is added to the egg whites at the foamy stage.
4. Bake the soufflé at 400° for 15 minutes. Reduce the oven temperature to 375° and bake it for an additional 25 minutes.

Hollandaise, Béarnaise, and Mayonnaise

Hollandaise sauce is made from warmed egg yolks, lemon juice, and butter. Béarnaise sauce is a specially flavored hollandaise. Mayonnaise is made by beating salad oil into egg yolks and lemon juice or vinegar.

All of these sauces are the permanent suspension of a fat in a liquid, with egg yolk acting as the stabilizing agent. The egg yolk separates or suspends tiny droplets of oil (or butter) in the liquid (water, vinegar, or lemon juice) so they cannot rejoin each other to form larger and larger drops of oil. This permanent suspension of fat in liquid is called emulsion.

An oil and vinegar salad dressing mixed in a bottle is a perfect example of an oil-liquid suspension that is not permanent. When the bottle is shaken, the oil and liquid mix together. As soon as the shaking motion is discontinued they separate again.

To make one of these sauces is really very simple. The egg yolk and liquid are mixed together, and the oil is gradually beaten in. The beating process breaks the oil into fine droplets. Occasionally the oil may separate out or refuse to be broken into fine droplets. When this happens, don't throw away the sauce. It can almost certainly be saved. Remedies are given at the end of each recipe.

Don't add increased amounts of oil to the sauce or it will eventually become so thick it can be cut with a knife. This is obviously not a desirable sauce. We also recommend that you never make these sauces on a humid day.

Cooked Hollandaise Sauce

*Quantity: Three-quarters cup
sauce*

Ingredients
½ cup butter (8 tablespoons)
2 extra large egg yolks
¼ teaspoon salt
    dash of cayenne pepper
1 tablespoon lemon juice

Utensils
set of measuring spoons
2 small bowls
double boiler
wire whisk
juicer
hot pad

Procedure
1. Read the chapter introduction.
2. Cut the butter into eight pieces and set them in a warm place to soften but not melt.
3. Separate the eggs into the 2 small bowls. Refrigerate or freeze the whites for future use. Set the yolks aside.
4. Squeeze and measure out the lemon juice.
5. Set out all other utensils and ingredients in a convenient working space.
6. Fill the bottom half of the double boiler with water and heat the water over a low flame until it begins to steam.
□ The water should never simmer or boil.
7. When the butter is very soft, you are ready to begin cooking the hollandaise.
8. Put the egg yolks in the top of the double boiler and place them over the hot water. Beat them with the wire whisk until they be-

come thick. This should take about 1 minute.
9. Add the lemon juice, salt, and pepper and beat the yolks for half a minute.
10. Beat the butter into the egg yolks 1 tablespoon at a time. When you have added the last bit of butter, the sauce should be thick and creamy.
11. Remove from the heat and serve at once. You may keep the sauce warm for an hour if you cover the pan and place it over warm, not hot, water in the bottom of the double boiler.
12. The sauce may be refrigerated for 2 days or frozen for longer periods of time. To reconstitute the stored sauce, place 2 tablespoons of the sauce in the top of the double boiler and fill the bottom of the double boiler with hot, not boiling, water. Beat the small amount of sauce with a wire whisk. Beat in the balance of the sauce tablespoon by tablespoon.

Hollandaise remedies
1. If the sauce is too thick, add 1 or 2 tablespoons of hot water.
2. If the sauce will not thicken, put 1 teaspoon of lemon juice and 1 tablespoon of sauce in a warm mixing bowl. Beat the mixture with a wire whisk until it thickens. Add the remaining sauce a teaspoon at a time, beating each addition until the sauce has thickened.
3. If the sauce curdles, beat in 1 tablespoon of cold water. If the sauce is still curdled, use Remedies Step 2.

Béarnaise Sauce

Quantity: Three-quarters cup
sauce

Ingredients

½ cup butter (8 tablespoons)
3 extra large egg yolks
3 tablespoons white wine vine-
    gar
3 tablespoons dry white wine
¼ teaspoon salt
¼ teaspoon pepper
1 tablespoon finely chopped
    green onions
1 teaspoon finely chopped
    fresh tarragon or ½ tea-
    spoon dried tarragon
1 tablespoon finely chopped
    fresh parsley

Procedure

1. Read the chapter introduction.
2. Clean and finely chop the onions, parsley, and tarragon. Measure and put them in the small
saucepan. Measure and add vinegar and wine. Boil the mixture until it is reduced to about 2 tablespoons. Remove from the heat,
strain out the herbs, and measure
2 tablespoons of the liquid.
3. Follow the directions for
Cooked Hollandaise Sauce using
the liquid from Step 2 instead of
lemon juice.

Blender Hollandaise Sauce

Quantity: *Three-quarters cup sauce*

Ingredients
½ cup butter
3 extra large egg yolks
¼ teaspoon salt
  dash of pepper
2 tablespoons lemon juice

Special utensil
electric blender

Procedure
1. Read the chapter introduction.
2. Plan to have all the ingredients at room temperature when you are ready to begin. Separate the eggs while they are cold. Refrigerate the whites for future use.
3. Squeeze and measure out the lemon juice.
4. Melt the butter in the small saucepan over a low heat until it begins to foam. Set it next to the blender.
5. Place the egg yolks, salt, pepper, and lemon juice in the blender and blend at high speed for 30 seconds. The mixture will become thick and foamy.

6. Remove the clear plastic centerpiece from the lid of the blender and place the lid on the blender container. Turn the blender on to high speed and begin pouring the butter in a very thin stream into the egg yolk mixture through the small opening in the lid.
□ The lid will prevent the butter from splattering outside of the blender container.
7. Continue adding the butter in a thin stream until it has been completely absorbed by the hollandaise mixture in the blender. The hollandaise should be very thick at this point. Serve the sauce at once or place it in a pan of warm, not hot, water for no longer than 1 hour.

Hollandaise remedy
If the sauce refused to thicken while you added the butter, pour the sauce out of the blender container. Replace the empty container and lid and turn the blender on to high. Pour the unthickened sauce into the blender in a thin, steady stream. It should thicken.

Blender Mayonnaise

Quantity: One and one-half cups mayonnaise

Ingredients
1 cup fresh safflower oil
2 extra large egg yolks
½ teaspoon salt
¼ teaspoon dry mustard
2 tablespoons lemon juice

Special utensil
electric blender

Procedure
1. Read the chapter introduction.
2. Plan to have all the ingredients at room temperature when you are ready to begin. Separate the eggs while they are cold. Refrigerate the whites for future use.
3. Squeeze and measure out the lemon juice.
4. Measure out the oil in the glass measuring cup and set it next to the blender.
5. Place the egg yolks, salt, and mustard in the blender and blend at high speed for 30 seconds. The mixture will become thick and foamy.
6. Add the lemon juice and blend for a few seconds.
7. Remove the clear plastic centerpiece from the lid of the blender and place the lid on the blender container.
8. Turn the blender on to high speed and begin pouring the oil in a very thin stream into the egg yolk mixture through the small opening in the lid.
□ The lid will prevent the oil from splattering outside of the blender container.
9. Continue adding the oil in a thin stream until it has been completely absorbed by the mayonnaise mixture in the blender. The mayonnaise should be very thick at this point. Stop the blender and transfer the mayonnaise to a glass container. Store the mayonnaise in the refrigerator at all times.

Mayonnaise remedies
1. If the mayonnaise is too thick, add 1 tablespoon of lemon juice.
2. If the mayonnaise will not thicken, remove it from the blender. Place a fresh egg yolk and a teaspoon of lemon juice in the container and blend at high speed for a few seconds. Add the unthickened mayonnaise in a thin stream while blending at high speed. The mayonnaise should thicken.

Chantilly Sauce

Quantity: One cup sauce

Ingredients
½ cup butter
3 extra large egg yolks
¼ cup whipped cream
¼ teaspoon salt
   dash of pepper
2 tablespoons lemon juice

Special utensil
electric blender

Procedure
Follow the directions for Blender Hollandaise Sauce. Fold in the whipped cream just before the sauce is served.

Sauces, Gravies, and Puddings

The recipes in this group can be real troublemakers. They are all based on the ability of a starch to thicken a liquid. The most outstanding examples of this principle are white sauces, brown sauces, gravies, and cornstarch puddings.

Mastery of sauce cookery should be a part of every good cook's repertoire. A fine sauce is the crowning glory of a meal, and the basis for many dishes. A thin white sauce becomes a cream soup. Gravies and sauces that accompany meat, fish, vegetable, and dessert dishes are all made from a sauce of medium thickness. A soufflé is a combination of an egg foam and a thick white sauce. Cornstarch pudding is an example of an extremely thick sauce.

Starches are preferred to eggs as a thickener for several reasons. They store well. They have very little flavor. A small amount will thicken a large amount of liquid. For all these reasons, starches are less expensive and often preferable to egg yolks.

The starch thickeners used in this book are flour and cornstarch. Flour makes an opaque sauce. It is the most durable thickener, being able to withstand heat for long periods of time without disintegrating. Cornstarch will dissolve in a liquid more easily than flour, but it is much more fragile. Cornstarch becomes heavy and gummy when it is cooked for extended periods of time. It makes a clear sauce when it is mixed with a clear liquid. The other common thickeners are arrowroot, tapioca, potato starch, and rice starch. All of these starches are very tender and disintegrate very easily when they are heated to the boiling point or allowed to simmer for long periods of time.

Combining a starch with a liquid successfully is the first and most difficult lesson in starch cookery. If the two are mixed incorrectly, disagreeable lumps occur because the particles of starch swell before they can be thoroughly dispersed in the liquid. There are three ways that lumping can be avoided:

1. A cold liquid is always added to a starch. Absolutely never add a hot liquid. This is common to all recipes using starch as a thickener.
2. The starch is thoroughly mixed with melted fat before adding the cold liquid. This principle is utilized in white sauces.
3. The starch is mixed with the other dry ingredients to separate the starch particles before the cold liquid is added. An example of this is a cornstarch pudding.

After the starch is dissolved, it must be cooked for 5 minutes or the finished product will have a raw starch taste. Flour and cornstarch must also be heated to the boiling point for maximum thickening to occur.

Starch-thickened liquids should never be cooked in a double boiler, though you will find many recipes directing you to cook them that way. The double boiler cooks the starch too slowly and will cause it to become heavy and gummy. The starch should be cooked in a heavy pan placed directly over the heat. For maximum thickening and the best consistency, starch is cooked quickly over high heat.

Starch mixtures must be stirred constantly. They will thicken more quickly around the sides and bottom of the pan, causing lumps in the finished sauce if it is not stirred.

Never add more sugar than the recipe calls for. Excessive amounts of sugar will reduce the thickening power of the starch.

Always add acids, like lemon juice, to the starch mixture after the thickening is completed. If the acid is added before thickening, the mixture will not thicken as well.

Sauces and Gravies

A white sauce is made from equal parts of flour and melted fat mixed into a paste called roux. The roux is then diluted with a cold liquid and cooked until it thickens into a sauce.

The basic white sauce may take on a multitude of disguises. A variety of liquids can be used in the sauce, each contributing a characteristic flavor. Or, the sauce can be changed with seasonings. But the final enhancement of the sauce is the chopped meat, seafood, vegetables, or grated cheese added after the sauce has thickened.

A brown sauce has a unique flavor. It is made from a roux that is cooked until it turns a light brown. The brown sauce is the basis for many complicated French sauces, which provide enough subject matter for another entire book. We describe here only the most simple brown sauce to help you master the basic principle behind the sauce. It is important to note that the browning process reduces the thickening power of the flour. Consequently, a brown sauce will use slightly more flour than a white sauce of comparable thickness.

Gravies utilize the same mixing and cooking procedures as a sauce. Meat drippings replace the butter in the Basic White Sauce, and water usually replaces the milk.

A good sauce is smooth and free of lumps. It is the appropriate thickness when it is hot. (Sauces thicken as they cool.) There is no fat film over the surface of the sauce.

There are two additional helpful points to remember in sauce cookery: Any fat which is to be added to the sauce beyond the prescribed equal parts of fat to flour should be beaten into the thickened sauce just before it is served. And a sauce made from equal parts of fat and flour which does develop a fat film may be corrected by carefully adding liquid to the sauce. The film formed because too much liquid evaporated from the sauce while it was cooking.

Thin White Sauce

(used as a base for
cream soups)

Quantity: One cup sauce

Ingredients
1 tablespoon butter
1 tablespoon all-purpose flour
1 cup cold milk
¼ teaspoon salt
⅛ teaspoon pepper

Utensils
glass measuring cup
set of measuring spoons
medium saucepan
small heavy saucepan
wire whisk
kitchen timer
hot pad

Procedure

Preparation
1. Read the chapter introduction.
2. These ingredients do not need
to be at room temperature; as a
matter of fact, the milk should be
cold when you use it. Set out all
ingredients and utensils in a convenient working space.

Cooking
1. Measure the butter and melt it
in the saucepan over a low heat.
2. Measure out the flour and
stir it into the butter, making a
smooth paste. Set your timer for 5
minutes and continue cooking the
flour-butter mixture until the timer
goes off. Stir the mixture at a
slow, even rate during the entire
cooking time. This mixture is
known as a roux.
□ This cooking time is necessary
or the finished sauce will have a
raw flour taste.
□ Rapid or vigorous stirring destroys the thickening power of the
flour.
3. Measure the cold milk and
gradually stir it into the flour-butter mixture. Continue stirring until
the mixture is smooth and evenly
mixed. Turn the flame to medium
and cook the mixture for 3 minutes or until it just begins to boil.
Stir the mixture slowly and steadily as it cooks.
4. Remove the white sauce from
the stove and add the seasonings.
5. You may keep the sauce warm
for 1 hour by covering the saucepan with a tight-fitting lid and
placing it in a pan of hot water.

Cream of Celery Soup

Quantity: Four cups soup

Ingredients

White sauce
   3 tablespoons butter
   3 tablespoons all-purpose flour
   3 cups milk
1½ teaspoons salt
   ¼ teaspoon pepper

Other ingredients
   ½ cup water
   2 cups finely chopped celery
   ¼ cup finely chopped onion

Procedure

1. Read the chapter introduction.
2. Set out all ingredients and utensils in a convenient working space.
3. Clean the celery and chop the stalks very finely with a sharp French knife. Measure out 2 cups of chopped celery. Chop and measure the onions.
4. Measure out the ½ cup of water and bring it to a boil in the small saucepan. Add the chopped onion and celery. Cover the pan and simmer over a low flame for 5 minutes. Remove from the heat and set aside.

☐ Do not drain off any water left after the vegetables are cooked.
☐ Watch the pan carefully as the water will be nearly evaporated when the vegetables are cooked.
5. Prepare a white sauce using the proportions of ingredients in this recipe and the directions for the Thin White Sauce.
6. To shorten the cooking time of the sauce, you may scald 2 cups of the milk before adding them to the sauce. The first cup of milk should be added cold.
7. Combine the white sauce and the cooked celery-onion mixture. Taste the soup and carefully correct the seasoning. Bring to a boil and serve at once. Beat the soup with a wire whisk for a minute before transferring it to serving bowls. The foam from the beating will retard the formation of a skin on the surface of the soup. Or, a spoonful of unsweetened whipped cream on the top of each bowl of soup will serve as a garnish and retard the skin formation.
☐ Never allow the soup to boil on the stove for more than 1 or 2 minutes. The soup will curdle.
☐ Always store cream soup in a tightly covered container.

Cream of Mushroom Soup

Quantity: *Four cups soup*

Ingredients

White sauce
- 3 tablespoons butter
- 3 tablespoons all-purpose flour
- 2¾ cups milk
- ¼ cup dry white wine
- 1 teaspoon salt
- ¼ teaspoon pepper
  dash of nutmeg

Other ingredients
- ½ cup water
- 2 tablespoons finely chopped onion
- 2 cups finely chopped mushrooms
- 1 tablespoon chopped fresh parsley

Procedure
Follow the directions for Cream of Celery Soup. Add the wine with the scalded milk.

Cream of Tomato Soup

Quantity: Four cups soup

Ingredients

White sauce
2 tablespoons butter
3 tablespoons all-purpose flour
3 cups whole milk
1 teaspoon salt
¼ teaspoon pepper

Other ingredients
2 cups puréed tomato
   (approximately 3 medium-size tomatoes)
¼ teaspoon onion powder
¼ teaspoon baking soda

Special utensil
electric blender

Procedure
1. Read the chapter introduction.
2. Set out all ingredients and utensils in a convenient working space.
3. Bring about 4 cups of water to a boil in a medium saucepan. Drop the tomatoes into the boiling water for 1 minute. Remove them from the water to the bowl with a slotted spoon. Run cold water over the tomatoes. Puncture the tomato skin with a knife, and it will easily peel off the tomato. Cut the tomatoes into quarters and remove the seeds. Purée the peeled, seeded tomato pieces in an electric blender. Measure out 2 cups of puréed tomatoes.
4. Prepare a white sauce using the proportions of ingredients in this recipe and the directions for a Thin White Sauce. Cover the sauce and keep the sauce hot while you heat the tomato pulp in a small saucepan. Measure and stir the baking soda and onion powder into the tomato purée. Gradually beat the hot tomato purée into the hot white sauce using a wire whisk. Taste the soup, carefully correct the seasoning, and serve at once. A spoonful of unsweetened whipped cream on the top of each bowl of soup will serve as a garnish and retard any skin formation.
□ The soup will curdle if you beat the white sauce into the soup.
□ To shorten the cooking time of the sauce, you may scald 2 cups of the milk before adding it to the sauce. The first cup of milk should be added cold.

James Pulliam's Clam Soup

Quantity: *Four cups soup*

Ingredients

White sauce
   1 tablespoon butter
   1 tablespoon all-purpose flour
   3 cups milk
   1 teaspoon salt
   ¼ teaspoon pepper

Other ingredients
   1½ cups water
   ½ cup clam broth
   ½ cup minced clams
   1 medium-size potato
   ½ cup finely chopped onion
   4 slices thick bacon
      chopped fresh parsley

Special utensils
frying pan

Procedure
1. Read the chapter introduction.
2. Set out all ingredients and utensils in a convenient working space.
3. Clean, chop, and measure the onion. Chop a handful of parsley. Set both aside.
4. Cut the bacon into small pieces. Fry the bacon to a crisp golden brown. Remove it from the pan and drain it on paper toweling. Set it aside.

5. Sauté the chopped onion pieces in the bacon grease over a low flame until they are transparent and brown on the edges. Pour off excess grease. Set the onions aside.
6. Peel and dice the potato into ¼-inch cubes. Boil the potatoes in the 1½ cups of water until they are tender but still firm. Drain off the water and set aside.
□ Do not overcook the potato cubes or they will become mushy and break apart.
7. Prepare a white sauce using the proportions of ingredients in this recipe and the directions for the Thin White Sauce.
8. To shorten the cooking time of the white sauce, you may scald 2 cups of the milk before adding it to the sauce. The first cup of milk should be added cold.
9. Combine the white sauce, clams, clam broth, potato cubes, bacon pieces, and onion. Taste the soup and correct the seasoning. Bring to a boil and serve at once. Garnish each bowl of soup with chopped fresh parsley.
□ Never allow the soup to boil on the stove for more than 1 or 2 minutes. The soup will curdle.
□ Always store cream soup in a tightly covered container.

Medium White Sauce

Quantity: One cup sauce

Ingredients
2 tablespoons butter
2 tablespoons all-purpose flour
1 cup cold milk
¼ teaspoon salt
⅛ teaspoon pepper

Utensils
glass measuring cup
set of measuring spoons
small heavy saucepan
wire whisk
hot pad

Procedure

Preparation
1. Read the chapter introduction.
2. These ingredients do not need to be at room temperature; as a matter of fact, the milk should be cold when you use it. Set out all ingredients and utensils in a convenient working space.

Cooking
1. Measure the butter and melt it in the saucepan over a low heat.
2. Measure out the flour and stir it into the butter, making a smooth paste. Set your timer for 5 minutes and continue cooking the flour-butter mixture until the timer goes off. Stir the mixture at a slow, even rate during the entire cooking time. This mixture is known as a roux.
□ This cooking time is necessary or the finished sauce will have a raw flour taste.
□ Rapid or vigorous stirring destroys the thickening power of the flour.
3. Measure the cold milk and gradually stir it into the flour-butter mixture. Continue stirring until the mixture is smooth and evenly mixed. Turn the flame to medium and cook the mixture for 3 minutes or until it just begins to boil. Stir the mixture slowly and steadily as it cooks.
4. Remove the white sauce from the stove and add the seasonings.
5. You may keep the sauce warm for 1 hour by covering the saucepan with a tight-fitting lid and placing it in a pan of hot water.

Rich White Sauce

Quantity: One cup sauce

Ingredients

White sauce
  2 tablespoons butter
  2 tablespoons all-purpose flour
  1 cup cold half-and-half
  ¼ teaspoon salt
  ⅛ teaspoon pepper

Other ingredients
  1 egg yolk

Procedure
1. Prepare the sauce following the directions for Medium White Sauce. Remove the pan from the stove.
2. Separate the egg into 2 small bowls. Refrigerate or freeze the white for future use.
3. Beat 1 tablespoon of sauce into the egg yolk. Beat another tablespoon into the yolk. Repeat this process three more times.
4. Stir the sauce-egg yolk mixture into the rest of the sauce. Cook over low heat until the sauce begins to boil. Serve at once.

Cheese Sauce

Quantity: One cup sauce

Ingredients

White sauce
  2 tablespoons butter
  2 tablespoons all-purpose flour
  1 cup cold milk
  ¼ teaspoon salt
  ⅛ teaspoon pepper
    few drops of Worcestershire
      sauce

Other ingredients
  ¼ cup grated cheese
    dash cayenne pepper
  ½ teaspoon dry mustard (optional)

Procedure
1. Read the chapter introduction.
2. Grate and measure the cheese. Set it aside.
3. Prepare the sauce following the directions for Medium White Sauce. Remove the pan from the stove.
4. Stir in the grated cheese, cayenne pepper, and mustard. Serve at once.
□ Never boil or cook cheese at high temperatures. It will become stringy and rubbery.

Wine Sauce

Quantity: One cup sauce

Ingredients
3 tablespoons butter
3 tablespoons all-purpose flour
½ cup dry white wine or sherry
½ cup cold, grease-free chicken
    broth
¼ teaspoon salt
⅛ teaspoon pepper

Procedure
Prepare the sauce following the directions for Medium White Sauce. Combine the broth and wine and substitute them for the milk.

Velouté Sauce

Quantity: One cup sauce

Ingredients
2 tablespoons butter
2 tablespoons all-purpose flour
1 cup cold, grease-free chicken
    broth
¼ teaspoon salt
⅛ teaspoon pepper

Procedure
Prepare the sauce following the directions for Medium White Sauce. The chicken broth replaces the milk.

Cream Gravy

Quantity: *One cup gravy*

Ingredients
2 tablespoons meat drippings
2 tablespoons all-purpose flour
1 cup cold milk
¼ teaspoon salt
⅛ teaspoon pepper

Procedure
1. Read the chapter introduction.
2. Remove the meat from the pan to a serving plate or platter. Cover to keep it warm.

3. Remove all the meat drippings from the pan. Measure out 2 tablespoons of drippings for every cup of gravy you wish and return the drippings to the pan.
4. Prepare the gravy following the directions for Medium White Sauce. Remember to increase the amount of other ingredients if you increase the amount of drippings.
□ If you wish to add the meat juices (other than drippings) to the gravy, you must first dissolve the flour in a small amount of cold milk. Then you may add meat juices to the roux.

Clear Gravy

Quantity: *Three-quarters cup gravy*

Ingredients
1 tablespoon meat drippings or butter
2 teaspoons cornstarch
1 cup cold meat stock or ¼ cup cold water and ¾ cup hot meat stock
¼ teaspoon salt
⅛ teaspoon pepper

Procedure
1. Read the chapter introduction.
2. Measure out the cornstarch, salt, and pepper into the small saucepan. Measure out the 1 cup cold meat stock or ¼ cup cold water in the glass measuring cup.

Gradually stir it into the cornstarch mixture and continue stirring until all the cornstarch is dissolved in the liquid. There should be no lumps.
3. If you used the cold water to dissolve the cornstarch, stir in the remaining hot meat stock.
4. Cook over a medium heat, stirring constantly at a medium speed, until the mixture thickens. It will take about 10 minutes to completely thicken and cook the cornstarch.
□ Vigorous stirring will reduce thickening power of the cornstarch.
5. Stir in the meat drippings or butter. Serve at once.

Thick White Sauce

Quantity: *One cup sauce*

Ingredients
- 3 tablespoons butter
- 3 tablespoons all-purpose flour
- 1 cup cold milk
- ¼ teaspoon salt
- ⅛ teaspoon pepper

Procedure

Preparation
1. Read the chapter introduction.
2. These ingredients do not need to be at room temperature; as a matter of fact, the milk should be cold when you use it. Set out all ingredients and utensils in a convenient working space.

Cooking
1. Measure out the butter and melt it in the saucepan over a low heat.
2. Measure out the flour and stir it into the butter, making a smooth paste. Set your timer for 5 minutes and continue cooking the flour-butter mixture until the timer goes off. Stir the mixture at a slow, even rate during the entire cooking time. This mixture is known as a roux.
□ This cooking time is necessary or the finished sauce will have a raw flour taste.
□ Rapid or vigorous stirring destroys the thickening power of the flour.
3. Measure out the cold milk and gradually stir it into the flour-butter mixture. Continue stirring until the mixture is smooth and evenly mixed. Turn the flame to medium and cook the mixture for 3 minutes or until it just begins to boil. Stir the mixture slowly and steadily as it cooks.
4. Remove the white sauce from the stove and add the seasonings.
5. You may keep the sauce warm for 1 hour by covering the saucepan with a tight-fitting lid and placing it in a pan of hot water.

Simple Brown Sauce

Quantity: Two cups brown sauce

Ingredients
- 2 tablespoons butter
- 3 tablespoons all-purpose flour
- 2 cups canned beef bouillon
- ½ cup dry white wine
- ¼ teaspoon salt
- ⅛ teaspoon pepper
- 3 tablespoons finely chopped onion
- 3 tablespoons finely chopped carrot
- 1 tablespoon finely chopped celery
- 1 teaspoon chopped fresh parsley
- ½ teaspoon finely chopped fresh thyme or ⅛ teaspoon dried thyme

Special utensils
strainer

Procedure
1. Read the chapter introduction.
2. Clean and chop finely the onion, carrot, celery, parsley, and thyme. Measure each one and put them in a small saucepan. In a glass measuring cup, measure the dry white wine and beef bouillon and add to the vegetable mixture.

Simmer these ingredients for 20 minutes. Strain out the vegetables and reserve the liquid for your sauce.

□ Don't substitute consommé for bouillon. The flavor of consommé is not the same.

3. Cool the liquid before making the sauce.
4. Measure the butter and melt it in a saucepan over a low heat. Measure out 3 tablespoons of flour and stir it into the butter making a smooth paste. Set the saucepan over a medium heat and cook the paste until it turns a nut brown. This should take about 8 minutes.

□ When flour is browned, some of its thickening power is lost. This is the reason for the change in the butter-flour-liquid ratio.

5. Measure out 2¼ cups of the liquid (from step 2) in a glass measuring cup and gradually stir it into the browned paste. Continue stirring over a medium heat until the mixture is smooth and evenly mixed. Cook for 3 minutes, stirring slowly and steadily, until the sauce just begins to boil.
6. Remove the sauce from the stove, add the seasonings, and serve at once.

Brown Gravy

Quantity: One cup gravy

Ingredients
2 tablespoons meat drippings (fat)
3 tablespoons all-purpose flour
1 cup grease-free meat broth
¼ cup cold water
¼ teaspoon salt
⅛ teaspoon pepper

Procedure
1. Read the chapter introduction.
2. Remove the meat from the pan to a serving plate or platter. Cover to keep it warm.
3. Remove all the meat drippings from the pan. Measure out 2 tablespoons of fat for every cup of gravy you wish to make and return the fat to the pan.
4. Measure out 3 tablespoons of flour for every 2 tablespoons of drippings in the pan and stir the flour into the fat making a smooth paste. Set the pan on a medium flame and cook the flour-drippings paste until the flour turns a nut brown. This should take about 8 minutes.
☐ When the flour is browned, some of its thickening power is lost. This is the reason for the change in the fat-flour-liquid ratio.
5. Measure the cold water in a glass measuring cup and gradually stir it into the browned flour-fat mixture. Continue stirring over a medium flame until the mixture is smooth and evenly mixed. Gradually add the meat broth and cook the mixture for 3 minutes or until it just begins to boil. Stir the mixture slowly and steadily as it cooks.
6. Remove the gravy from the stove, add the seasonings, and serve at once.
☐ If you wish to add the meat juices (other than drippings) to the gravy, you must first dissolve the flour in a small amount of cold liquid. Then you may add the hot meat juices to the brown roux.

Puddings

Cornstarch pudding is a pleasing dessert that may be prepared in less than 15 minutes. As a matter of fact, it is actually as easy to make your own pudding from scratch as it is to use one of the packaged mixes. The homemade pudding not only has a superior flavor and consistency, but it is also less expensive. Follow the simple mixing and stirring techniques outlined in the recipe procedures and you will easily make a lovely pudding that is smooth, light, flavorful, and free of lumps.

Vanilla Pudding

Quantity: Two cups pudding

Ingredients
2 cups cold milk
3 tablespoons cornstarch
¼ cup white sugar
¼ teaspoon salt
1 tablespoon butter
1 teaspoon vanilla

Extra
whipped cream for garnish

Utensils
glass measuring cup
set of graduated metal measuring
   cups
set of measuring spoons
small mixing bowl
heavy medium saucepan with
   tight-fitting cover
wooden spoon
4 small serving dishes
kitchen timer
hot pad

Procedure
1. Read the chapter introduction.
2. Set out all ingredients and utensils in a convenient working space.
3. Measure out 1½ cups of the milk in the glass measuring cup

and pour the milk into the medium saucepan. Set the pan on the stove over a low heat and scald the milk (see page 29).
4. Measure out the cornstarch, sugar, and salt into the small mixing bowl. Stir to evenly mix them. (Sift, if necessary, to remove lumps.) Measure out the remaining ½ cup of milk. Gradually stir it into the dry ingredients; continue stirring until all the dry ingredients are dissolved in the milk. There should be no lumps.
5. Gradually add the cornstarch mixture to the hot scalded milk, stirring constantly until the mixture is completely and smoothly combined. Turn the heat up to medium and cook the pudding, stirring it constantly at a medium speed until it is very thick. At this time a spoon pulled broadside through the pudding will leave a distinct path. This should take about 5 minutes.
□ Vigorous stirring will reduce the thickening power of the cornstarch.
□ Cooking the pudding over a low heat for a longer period of time will make it heavy and gummy.

□ Discontinuing the stirring for even a minute will cause lumps, because the pudding is thickening more quickly around the bottom and sides of the pan.

6. Remove the thickened pudding from the stove. Stir in the butter. Cover the saucepan and cool the pudding for 30 minutes. Stir the vanilla into the cooled pudding.

□ The cover will prevent the formation of a skin on the surface of the pudding.

7. Pour the cooled pudding into the serving dishes and chill it in the refrigerator. Garnish with whipped cream just before serving.

Chocolate Pudding

Quantity: Two cups pudding

Ingredients
- 2 cups cold milk
- 3 tablespoons cornstarch
- ⅓ cup white sugar
- ¼ teaspoon salt
- 3 tablespoons unsweetened cocoa
- 1 tablespoon butter
- 1 teaspoon vanilla or peppermint extract

Extra
whipped cream for garnish

Procedure
Follow the directions for Vanilla Pudding. Combine the cocoa with the cornstarch, sugar, and salt before adding the milk. If a chocolate mint flavor is preferred, substitute the peppermint extract for the vanilla.

Butterscotch Pudding

Quantity: Two cups pudding

Ingredients

2 cups cold milk
4 tablespoons caramel syrup, page 160
3 tablespoons cornstarch
2 tablespoons white sugar
¼ teaspoon salt
1 tablespoon butter
1 teaspoon vanilla

Extra

caramel syrup and whipped cream for garnish

Procedure

Follow the directions for Vanilla Pudding. Combine the 4 tablespoons warm caramel syrup with the scalded milk. Reheat the remaining syrup, adding a tablespoon of hot water to thin it if necessary, and distribute the syrup evenly over the top of the pudding in the serving dishes. Garnish with whipped cream.

Bibliography

American Heritage editors. *The American Heritage Cook-book*. New York: American Heritage Book Publishing Co., Inc., 1964.

Bailey, Pearl. *Pearl's Kitchen*. New York: Harcourt Brace Jovanovich, Inc., 1973.

Beard, James; Glaser, Milton; Wolf, Burton; Kafka, Barbara Poses; Witty, Helen S.; and associates of the Good Cooking School. *The Cooks' Catalog*. New York: Harper & Row, 1975.

Berolzheimer, Ruth. *The American Woman's Cook Book*. Chicago: Consolidated Book Publishers, Inc., 1943.

Better Homes and Gardens' magazine editors. *Better Homes and Gardens New Cookbook*. Des Moines, Iowa: Meredith Press, 1969.

Bickel, Walter, and Kramer, René, eds. *L'Arte Della Pasticceria*. Translated by Laura Kurz Germi. Florence: Sansoni Publishers, 1971.

Braider, Carol. *The Grammer of Cooking*. New York: Holt Rinehart & Winston, 1974.

Bride's magazine editors. *Bride's Reference Book*. New York: M. Barrows & Co., Inc., 1956.

Casella, Dolores. *A World of Breads*. New York: David White Co., 1966.

Child, Julia; Bertholle, Louisette; and Beck, Simone. *Mastering the Art of French Cooking*. Vols. 1 and 2. New York: Alfred A. Knopf, 1966, 1970.

Claiborne, Craig. *The New York Times Menu Cook Book*. New York: Harper & Row, 1961.

Claiborne, Craig. *The New York Times Cook Book*. New York: Harper & Row, 1966.

Dowd, Mary T., and Dent, Alberta. *Elements of Food and Nutrition*. New York: John Wiley & Sons, Inc., 1945.

Griffin, Marjorie. *How to Cook*. New York: Hall Publishing Co., 1944.

Halliday, Evelyn G., and Noble, Isabel T. *Hows and Whys of Cooking*. Chicago: University of Chicago Press, 1928.

Herman, Judith, and Herman, Marguerite Shalett. *The Cornucopia*. New York: Harper & Row, 1973.

Heseltine, Marjorie, and Dow, Ula M. *Good Cooking—Made Easy and Economical*. New York: Houghton Mifflin Co., 1933.

Ladies of San Rafael, compilers. *San Rafael Cookbook*. California: 1906.

Laird, Jean E. *Around the Kitchen Like Magic*. New York: Harper & Row, 1968, 1969.

Lass, William. *Good Housekeeping's Guide for Young Home-makers.* New York: Harper & Row, 1966.

McCulley, Helen. *Things You've Always Wanted to Know About Food and Drink.* New York: Holt Rinehart & Winston, 1972.

McWilliams, Margaret. *Food Fundamentals.* New York: John Wiley & Sons, Inc., 1966.

Montagné, Prosper. *Larousse Gastronomique.* New York: Crown Publishers, 1961.

Rombauer, Irma S., and Becker, Marion Rombauer. *Joy of Cooking.* Indianapolis: The Bobbs-Merrill Co., 1967.

Sheppard, Ronald, and Newton, Edward. *The Story of Bread.* London: Routledge and Kegan Paul Ltd., 1957.

Stewart, John. *Bread and Baking.* London: Sir Isaac Pitman and Son, Ltd.

Taylor, Barbara Howland. *Mexico: Her Daily and Festive Breads.* Claremont, California: The Creative Press, 1969.

U. S. Department of Agriculture. *Breads, Cakes and Pies in Family Meals.* Home and Garden Bulletin 186. Prepared by the Consumer and Food Economics Research Division, Agricultural Research Service. Washington, D. C.: U. S. Government Printing Office, 1971.

Index